Samuel French Acting Edition

M000166545

The Incredibly Famous Willy Rivers

A Play

by Stephen Metcalfe

SAMUELFRENCH.COM   SAMUELFRENCH.CO.UK

FOR PRODUCTION ENQUIRIES

UNITED STATES AND CANADA
Info@SamuelFrench.com
1-866-598-8449

UNITED KINGDOM AND EUROPE
Plays@SamuelFrench.co.uk
020-7255-4302

Each title is subject to availability from Samuel French, depending upon country of performance. Please be aware that *THE INCREDIBLY FAMOUS WILLY RIVERS* may not be licensed by Samuel French in your territory. Professional and amateur producers should contact the nearest Samuel French office or licensing partner to verify availability.

MUSIC USE NOTE

Licensees are solely responsible for obtaining formal written permission from copyright owners to use copyrighted music in the performance of this play and are strongly cautioned to do so. If no such permission is obtained by the licensee, then the licensee must use only original music that the licensee owns and controls. Licensees are solely responsible and liable for all music clearances and shall indemnify the copyright owners of the play(s) and their licensing agent, Samuel French, against any costs, expenses, losses and liabilities arising from the use of music by licensees. Please contact the appropriate music licensing authority in your territory for the rights to any incidental music.

IMPORTANT BILLING AND CREDIT REQUIREMENTS

If you have obtained performance rights to this title, please refer to your licensing agreement for important billing and credit requirements.

WPA THEATRE PRESENTS
KYLE RENICK - ARTISTIC DIRECTOR

THE INCREDIBLY FAMOUS WILLY RIVERS

By Stephen Metcalfe
Directed by Stephen Zuckerman
Setting by James Fenhagen
Lighting by Richard Winkler
Costumes by Mimi Maxmen
Music by Denny McCormick
Sound by Aural Fixation

Cast in order of appearance

Willy Rivers	Jay O. Sanders
Suit	Hansford Rowe
Subway Girl #1	Elizabeth Berridge
Subway Girl #2	Kathy Rossetter
Mom	Lois Chiles
Friend	John Bedford-Lloyd
Friend's Wife	Elizabeth Berridge
Reporter	James McDaniel
Reporter	Lois Chiles
Beggar	John Bowman
Reporter	Elizabeth Berridge
Reporter	John Bedford-Lloyd
Anchorman	Dave Florek
Blonde	Kathy Rossetter
Announcer	Hansford Rowe
Goatman Jango	James McDaniel
TV Director	John Bedford-Lloyd
Actor	Dave Florek
Darlene	Lois Chiles
Gypsy Davie	John Bedford-Lloyd
Groupie	Elizabeth Berridge
Killer	John Bowman
Roadie	Dave Florek
Cop	James McDaniel
TV Show Host	John Bowman
Trenchcoat #1	Dave Florek
Trenchcoat #2	James McDaniel
Guard	James McDaniel
Husband	John Bedford-Lloyd
Paramedic	John Bowman
Paramedic	Dave Florek
Dad	Hansford Rowe

Time: The Present

Music Produced and Arranged by
Don Markowitz and Denny McCormick

Lyrics by Stephen Metcalfe

THE INCREDIBLY FAMOUS WILLY RIVERS

by

Stephen Metcalfe

Director	Jack O'Brien
Scenic Designer	Douglas W. Schmidt*
Costume Designer	Robert Blackman
Lighting Designer	David F. Segal
Sound Designer	Michael Holten
Original Music Created and Produced by	Donny Markowitz and Denny McCormick
Lyrics by	Stephen Metcalfe
Production Stage Manager	Douglas Pagliotti
Stage Manager	Diane F. DiVita

Cast of Characters
(In order of appearance)

Willy Rivers	Brian Kerwin
Suit/Gypsy Davey	Dann Florek
Subway Girl/Punk	Pippa Pearthree
Friend's Wife/Blonde	Lisa Dunsheath
Darlene	Sydney Lloyd-Smith
Friend/Blonde's Husband	William Anton
Anchorman/Actor	Dave Florek
Goatman Jango/Orderly	James McDaniel
Killer (Prisoner)	John Bowman
Dad/Beggar	Jonathan McMurtry*
Reporters, Security and others	Eric Grischkat, Mark Hofflund, Ric Oquita, Pamela Tomassetti

There will be one 15-minute interval.

*Associate Artist of the Old Globe Theatre

**This production of *The Incredibly Famous Willy Rivers*
is made possible in part by a generous grant from
Home Savings of America.**

OG-9

The play can be done with as few as four actors. In this case "the reporters" become one reporter. In any case actors should play multiple parts. For example:

Actor 1   Willy Rivers

Actor 2   Suit/Gypsy Davey

Actor 3   Subway Girl/Punk/Reporter

Actor 4   Friend/Reporter/Blonde's Husband

Actor 5   Television newsman/ The Actor

Actor 6   Friend's wife/Blonde

Actor 7   Darlene/Reporter

Actor 8   Goatman Jango/Reporter/Orderly

Actor 9   Dad/Reporter

Actor 10   The killer

THE INCREDIBLY FAMOUS WILLY RIVERS

ACT I

The faint sound of WHISTLING, of CHEERING, of STAMP-
ING FEET—APPLAUSE that suggests anticipation and
expectation. The sound is distant, muted; as if coming
through yards and yards of concrete; as if creeping through
from some distant place. The sound turns into a more
intense—what? Static? Applause? Feedback? All three?
Silence. And then a VOICE out of the blackness—
WILLY's voice.

WILLY. Ladies and gentlepeople, boys and those of the
female persuasion, if there are any dogs and cats in the
audience, they're invited to howwwwwllll....! I think we
can safely say—no, I don't think. I know—that he is a
legend in his own time. There is a lovely black and white
portrait of him on page 17 of your complimentary
souvenir program. A full color 24 by 36 inch poster of
him is on sale at convenient locations throughout the
arena and say, while you're out there, how bout a big
beer and a chili dog! Ladies and gentlemen, there ought
to be music and don't worry, there will be; ladies and
gentlemen, the incredibly famous Willy Rivers! *(The sound
again; STATIC, FEEDBACK, DISTORTED APPLAUSE.
LIGHTS have been slowly coming up. A MAN is sitting center.
The SOUND fades away. The MAN — WILLY — speaks.)*

WILLY. That was horrible. Let's get down! Let's get funky! Let's all get incredibly moist and sticky wet! Let's have a hometown welcome for your fave rave and mine, the incredibly famous Willy Rivers!

(The SOUND again. It is coming from a large cassette deck that WILLY is holding. He turns the sound to high and APPLAUSE on the verge of distortion reverberates throughout the house. He turns it off. SILENCE.)

WILLY. The incredible Willy Rivers! *(SOUND. Off.)* The famous Willy Rivers. *(Again. Off.)* Willy Rivers. *(Silence, and then softly.)* Oh, boy ... *(He rolls onto his back and stares at the ceiling.)* Hold on to your seats, I have a feeling it's going to be long one.

(A MAN in a suit enters.)

SUIT. Willy.
WILLY. Oh, oh. Devil with the blue suit on.
SUIT. Hello, Willy. Does anybody really know what time it is? I do. It's that time.
WILLY. No.
SUIT. Yes.
WILLY. Can't be time.
SUIT. Oh, but it is.
WILLY. No can be. I'm not ready.
SUIT. People tell me you're a problem, Willy. Are you a problem?
WILLY. *(Leaps to his feet.)* All right, let's get organized! I

want rabid fans on my left! I want screaming hordes on my right! Any girls ain't been under me, line up along the wall, I'll go as long as I can!

SUIT. You know what I am, Willy? I am a problem solver. Nothing I don't know, not a problem I can't solve.

WILLY. Where is my lucky jacket? That jacket's my trademark, jack! How am I supposed to convince anybody that a middle class kid from the heartland of America is misfitted, maladjusted and James Dean mean if I don't have my lucky jacket? That jacket has got wings on it, man! You know, I hope nobody went into their lifesavings for this nickel and dime extravaganza! I have never! Been treated! In first class! Like this! In my life!

SUIT. Willy.

WILLY. Sir?

SUIT. You cut the shit.

WILLY. *(WILLY seems to sag. He is terrified of something.)* I can't. Nothing feels right.

SUIT. People don't pay to hear excuses.

WILLY. It's like there's too much blood pumping through my body.

SUIT. Nerves. Nerves are to be expected.

WILLY. My back hurts. My throat and hands.

SUIT. That's all in your mind.

WILLY. It is not in my mind. My body predicts the weather and it is tellin me that the weather, man, bites the big one.

SUIT. And so?

WILLY. And so ... *(He rushes to his tape deck and puts on the headphones.)* You ever seen one a these? This is a super-deluxe, class A, top of the line, get down and boogie walkman. And that's what I'm gonna do. Walk, man.

SUIT. Take your time, Willy. Get it all out of your system.

WILLY. Can't hear you! You wanna talk to me you're gonna have to put it on a cassette and plug it in. Panasonic Willy Rivers! I bet God wears headphones.

SUIT. Just remember. You and I have a contract. I love contracts. They're so ... binding.

WILLY. What? I can see your lips move but I can't hear a thing. Speak no evil, see no evil and I can't hear no evil at all, man.

SUIT. Willy-Willy-Willy. I am so disappointed. It is time and everyone is ready except you.

WILLY. Hey, I was born ready, buddy.

SUIT. Ahh, you can hear me. I thought so. No more excuses. You're answering to me now. You'll hear your cue. You'll go on. *(Exiting)* Ladies and gentlemen, the incredibly famous Willy Rivers.

WILLY. No! Hey! *(psyching himself now)* Okay, man. A river flows through here and it's wild and fast and in places the whitewater leaps to fifty feet high. And the name of that river ... is Willy! Where's my guitar? Hey! How am I supposed to rock and roll without a guitar!? *(Pause. He sags, the false bravado gone.)* Lord, lord ... where am I gonna find the strength to do this?

(As if from a distant part of his mind: a GUITAR RIFF. It is violent, angry, on the edge of distortion.)

WILLY. *(softly, to himself)* Oh, it is absolutely amazing the things that flash across a man's mind when he feels like he's going down and under for the third time.

(Again: GUITAR RIFF.)

WILLY. It is amazing the things that flash across your mind.

(Still again: A GUITAR RIFF. Sustained. LIGHT change. FIGURES move and beckon to WILLY in the chaos. The guitar riff fades into the flashing lights and rising ROAR of a subway train. LIGHTS come up on WILLY and a YOUNG WOMAN in heavy make-up and tight clothing. She is reading a newspaper. She glances up at WILLY, looks him over; decides she likes what she sees. The YOUNG WOMAN speaks with a heavy Queens accent.)

GIRL. Hey. *(Pause)* Hey. *(Pause)* Hey. *(Pause)* Hey. *(She throws a hard elbow to get WILLY's attention.)* Hey, bozo! Don't ya see I'm talkin at ya, cheese!
WILLY. Sorry, what?
GIRL. Ya hear?
WILLY. Hear what?
GIRL. He! Is makin a comeback!
WILLY. Who?
GIRL. Ya so unread.
WILLY. Yeah, uh ... lately I don't have much time to read the papers.
GIRL. Tsk. Willy. *(Pause)*
WILLY. Willy who?
GIRL. Ya so ignorant! Willy Rivers!

WILLY. Yeah. How exciting. Willy Rivers. Jesus ... He's making a ... a what?

GIRL. Tsk. A comeback? *(showing him her paper)* From the tragic assassination attempt of catastrophic importance that nearly ended his career not to mention his friggin' life! Tsk. Why are the nice lookin' ones so dim? From the *shootin',* bozo. Where ya been keepin' ya' self, Alaska? I myself personally cried when he got shot.

WILLY. Yeah?

GIRL. Ya wanna know the truth, I died when he got shot. I bled fahr'm.

WILLY. Willy Rivers. He sure is very famous.

GIRL. And rich.

WILLY. Oh, yeah.

GIRL. And cute.

WILLY. Really?

GIRL. He's got one a them faces.

WILLY. The rich, famous and cute. *(WILLY and the GIRL sigh as one.)*

WILLY. They live the life, don't they?

GIRL. Celestial.

WILLY. Where'd we go wrong?

GIRL. Speak fah ya'self I'm sure. *(Pause)* Y'know, I saw'r him once. It was at the corner of 57th and Madison and he was getting out of a limo the size of a small third world country. That's how they travel, see. He looked nothin' like his photos but I figured he was incognito and so I knew it was him and I nearly peed. All cause I saw'r him.

WILLY. I touched him.

GIRL. No! Well ... if ya must know, I made it with him. It was under a table at the Hard Rock Cafe. It was 3 a.m. and I'd had about 14 kamikazes but I knew it was him by his tender touch. And I've thanked my lucky stars ever since. Because I made it with Willy Rivers.

WILLY. You too?

GIRL. *(a shocked gasp)* Ooh! No...

WILLY. Incredibly famous people of catastrophic importance, they're always swinging both ways.

GIRL. Well ... if ya must know, I personally had hoped to bear his child.

WILLY. I can't top that.

GIRL. I bet he remembers me.

WILLY. I bet you gave him something to remember.

GIRL. Oh, speak fah ya'self, I'm sure!

WILLY. Hey. Hey. Hey. Are you going to get tickets?

GIRL. One can only hope.

WILLY. What is it he does again?

GIRL. Well ... I ain't sure. But from what I understand, it tears ya heart out.

WILLY. He's good, huh?

GIRL. Tsk. Good-shmood! When there's the possibility that some psycho's gonna be packin a piece and blastin away; know what you are at? A multi-media event!

WILLY. The things *some* people charge admission to, huh?

GIRL. Ain't it the truth. Charge a guy and you's a whore. Add a gun an a few seats and you's a spectacular entertainment. *(Pause)*

WILLY. Do I know that. *(Pause)*

GIRL. Hey. Hey. HEY! Let's say the two of us stop off somewheres. I'll let you buy me a Lite beer from Miller.

(GUITAR RIFF! LIGHT change to WILLY with an electric guitar, trying to shape his left hand onto the neck of the guitar, trying to play. He groans in frustration. SUIT enters.)

SUIT. Practicing?

WILLY. I started off playing to records. Man, I'd turn the stereo up to a thousand and I'd dance with that first guitar of mine like it was my baby. Mom had a headache from the mid sixties on. Why do you play the stereo so loud, Willy!? You're gonna ruin your eardrums! She never understood that loud is the only way rock and roll sounds good. She was also convinced I woulda turned out normal if the Beatles hadn't been on Ed Sullivan. She didn't think I did teenage things. Go out with a girl, Willy! Get her pregnant. Go total the car! Go protest something like all your other friends! Go protest traffic lights, doberman pinchers. Go protest bell bottom pants! My mom prayed for a moments peace. Now my dad, my dad sorta knew how much it all meant to me. Course he didn't have to listen to it all day long. But he'd come home and let Mom blow off steam for awhile and then he'd come down to the basement and he'd look at the posters I'd taped to the walls, black light crazy shit, and he'd turn to me and he'd say, go for it, Willy. For your mom's sake, go for it quietly but go for it. My dad ... he was a fan.

(He strikes a chord. It sounds rough and tinny.)

WILLY. That was an A chord, man. The perfect A chord.

SUIT. I'm sure it would be if it weren't for the nerve damage.

WILLY. I learned a chord a day. Perfect chords. I practiced till my fingers bled. All that practice ... And man? I can't play worth a damn any more.

SUIT. Willy, you're a headliner now. You don't have to play. Others will play for you. All you have to do is stand there and look good.

WILLY. Hey ... maybe I should mouth the words too?

SUIT. I can arrange that if you like.

WILLY. You're never gonna understand. When you play the sound right, it's like stepping into another plane of existence, man. Your body is pistons, tubes, valves. You're aware of rods flowing into cylinders, of liquid seeping from chamber into chamber, of billows as they fill and empty, of life, man! You're aware of the tiny delicate to the pulse of a beat. You hear with your heart when you play, man. The music speaks words, man. You are, man. Man!

SUIT. Willy-baby-hunkie-dorie-sweetheart-kid.

WILLY. Yeah?

SUIT. That is a crock of shit and you know it.

WILLY. Yeah.

SUIT. I've been thinking. It's something I do. This is your show. Your comeback. You should be surrounded by people who care about you, by people who supported you when you were nothing special.

WILLY. Yeah?

SUIT. I was thinking it would be nice if you invited some. People who care about you, I mean. Unless, of course, you want me to go out and hire some professionals?

WILLY. No ... I mean, hey. I got people who care about me. I got good people.

SUIT. That's fine. The mark of a man is the people who care about him, am I right?

WILLY. Right.

SUIT. Right. On us, Willy, this is the big leagues, spare no expense. Invite anyone you want.

WILLY. Who...

SUIT. Who should you invite? I thought I made that clear. Your friends.

(He exits. LIGHT change. GUITAR RIFF. PEOPLE step out of the shadows. WILLY seems frozen. They slowly retreat.

LIGHTS to WILLY and a MAN in tennis whites. The MAN is holding a tennis racquet and bag. WILLY and the MAN are sitting, laughing uproariously. The laughter fades to nervous silence. The MAN keeps glancing at his wristwatch.)

FRIEND. So. Huh?

WILLY. Yeah.

FRIEND. Unbelievable.

WILLY. Yeah.

FRIEND. Such a long time.

WILLY. Too long.

FRIEND. Yeah. Hey, you get that card I sent you?

WILLY. Card?

FRIEND. Yeah. A Christmas card. Me, the wife, the kid, y'know, the dog, the cat, the tree. Everybody smiling. You didn't get that card?

WILLY. No.

FRIEND. It was a nice card.

WILLY. Sounds like it.

FRIEND. It wasn't cheap.

WILLY. They aren't.

FRIEND. Living color. Years from now, people will look at that card and say, will you look at that?

WILLY. So lifelike. So real.

FRIEND. Yeah.

WILLY. Everybody's old or dead now. *(Pause. They nod at each other, silent. The FRIEND glances at his watch.)*

FRIEND. My ride's due at any time.

WILLY. We can talk till he gets here.

FRIEND. He'll beep. I'll have to go right out.

WILLY. Fine. You drop by, you take your chances. I just wanted to say hello.

FRIEND. I appreciate it. A guy like you. When he beeps though, I'll have to run.

WILLY. Don't want to keep a person waiting.

FRIEND. Specially a doubles partner. Specially a doubles partner with a good overhead. Hey, my wife'll be home soon. I bet she'd love to chat. You know something? She never believes it when I tell her that we were best friends in high school.

WILLY. Boy, will she be surprised!

FRIEND. She's crazy about success. Especially overnight success. *(Pause. They nod at each other in silence. The FRIEND glances at his watch and smiles.)*

WILLY. How's your game?

FRIEND. Fine.

WILLY. Good. *(A beat)* Play a lot?

FRIEND. Yeah, I do.

WILLY. Great.

FRIEND. About eight or ten hours a day.

WILLY. That's a lot.

FRIEND. Except Tuesdays.

WILLY. Sorry?

FRIEND. Unemployment on Tuesdays. Yeah, for awhile I was looking for a job but then I decided, what the hell, 150 a week, tax free, doing nothing.

WILLY. You'd be hard pressed to do better than that working hard at something you hated.

FRIEND. Exactly. So I don't. I play tennis.

WILLY. You must be getting good.

FRIEND. I am. Topspin.

WILLY. Sorry?

FRIEND. Topspin. Topspin is the key to good groundstrokes. Gives you room to clear the net, keeps the ball safely within the baselines. Topspin. Topspin is the key to control.

WILLY. Sounds to me like topspin is the key to life. *(Pause)*

FRIEND. So!! You gettin any!!?

WILLY. Uh...

FRIEND. You are, aren't you! God, times have changed. Double dates, remember? A little nookie at the drive-in movies.

WILLY. Me in the backseat, you in the front.

FRIEND. Second base, bare tit, huh? Third base, a little sticky finger! Huh? Huh!?

WILLY. Christ, old friends.

FRIEND. Yeah.

WILLY. Old friends are the best friends.

FRIEND. Yeah.

WILLY. Shared experiences. That's what old friends have. They don't have to explain things, they know.

FRIEND. Hey, when you got shot? It was like I got shot. I wanted to get in touch.

WILLY. You didn't.

FRIEND. *(with vast, good humor)* Who the hell would have ever thought anybody'd want to shoot you, huh?

WILLY. Not me.

FRIEND. You certainly were on the outskirts in high school.

WILLY. Off in my own little world, yeah.

FRIEND. You want to know the truth, people thought you were stuck up. They thought your head was in the clouds. If you want to know the truth—

WILLY. I don't.

FRIEND. Everybody thought you were a twerp!

WILLY. Huh.

FRIEND. Guys always asked me why I let you hang with me. I mean, you remember who was voted most likely to succeed, don't you?

WILLY. You.

FRIEND. Me. I mean, you?

WILLY. Willy Rivers is weird, they'd say.

FRIEND. And they were right!

WILLY. I was.

FRIEND. You were! But hey, we were friends!

WILLY. Are.

FRIEND. And look at you now, huh? Hey! What are you worth?

WILLY. I, uh ... don't know.

FRIEND. That much, huh? Well, you deserve it. Getting shot. How do you put a dollar value on that? It's mindless entertainment. Mindless entertainment is priceless. It keeps you from thinking. I play tennis? I have a litany. Only the ball, only the ball, only the ball. It keeps me from thinking of other things. A kid could get hit by a truck in the parking lot, I wouldn't notice, that's how good my concentration is. Go ahead, say something to me, say something. *(He scoops up his racquet and takes a stance as if he's returning serve. It's as if he goes into a trance.)*

FRIEND. *(like a mantra)* Only the ball. Only the ball. Only the ball.

WILLY. I feel so alone.

FRIEND. Only the ball. *(snapping out of it)* Did you say something?

WILLY. Yes.

FRIEND. I didn't hear you! Concentration! What'd you say?

WILLY. I feel so alone.

FRIEND. You should. Life! It's a games of singles.

(Pause) Hey. Do you want to know something? My wife. She'd like to go to bed with you. Yeah. She said so. When I tell her we were friends once?

WILLY. We still are.

FRIEND. She says, boy, I'd crawl on my belly for a chance to fuck him. He was a twerp, I say. He could twerp me anytime, she says.

WILLY. People say funny things.

FRIEND. I don't laugh.

WILLY. People say things they don't really mean. Your wife, she doesn't even know me.

FRIEND. That's what she likes about you. You're anything she wants you to be.

(A BEEP)

FRIEND. There he is!

WILLY. Your ride!

FRIEND. Been great to see you. Stay as long as you want and come again but call first, okay?

WILLY. I will.

FRIEND. Bye! *(He Exits.)*

WIFE. *(off)* I'm home!

FRIEND. *(off)* It's not my ride, it's only my wife! Honey, we have a guest! Do I have a surprise for you!

(He and his WIFE Enter. He has his hands over her eyes. She is wearing cover-alls and a hard hat.)

FRIEND. This! Is the incredibly famous Willy Rivers, honey! *(He pulls his hands away.)*

WILLY. Hi. It's very nice to meet you.

WIFE. Oh, my god.

WILLY. I've heard so much about you.

WIFE. I'm going to faint.

WILLY. So this is your little breadwinner, huh?

FRIEND. Yes, sir! How are things down at the Ford plant, dear?

WIFE. I'm going to die.

FRIEND. Sit down, old friend. Maybe the little woman will whip us some frozen egg rolls and jalepeno bean dip.

WILLY. Reminiscing sure is hard work!

WIFE. Ohhh ... *(Falls to her knees.)*

WILLY. She's exhausted.

FRIEND. Hard day on the assembly line, dear? Dear?

WILLY. She's a little hard of hearing.

FRIEND. Yeah, that Ford plant's noisy. *(The WIFE begins crawling on her belly towards WILLY.)*

WILLY. They're planning this big comeback for me and I wonder if you'd like to attend? *(The WIFE flips over on her bak and begins doing the backstroke.)*

WILLY. You and your wife. Seats and hotel rooms will be taken care of. You could meet some nice people.

FRIEND. I'd love to, buddy of mine. Unfortunately I have league, old buddy. Tennis. Tennis. Tennis league.

WILLY. I see. *(The WIFE is on her knees in front of WILLY, touching him to see if he's real.)*

FRIEND. If she's bothering you, Willy, just give her a solid smack on the snout with a rolled up newspaper.

(A HORN beeps.)

FRIEND. There he is! Great to see you, Willy. Be in touch, o.k.? And leave the little woman your mailing address, won'tcha? We're gonna be sure you get that Christmas card this year and god knows it'd be nice to get in touch if somebody tries to shoot you again! *(He kisses his wife on the top of the head.)* Don't wait up, dear, I'll be late. Bye! *(He Exits.)*

WIFE. Take me now before I die.

(GUITAR! LIGHT change. WILLY freezes. A MAN enters out of the shadows. Stops. Reaches beneath his jacket as if for a gun. And comes out with a notepad.)

REPORTER. Here he is! *(WILLY turns to flee as PEOPLE come running on from all directions. They're reporters and they thrust cassette recorders at WILLY, wave notebooks and pencils. WILLY keeps trying to push him away.)*

REPORTERS. *(ad libbing)* Willy! Willy! Question, Willy, question! Here, Willy! Question! Question! Your scars! Show us your scars! We want to see your scars!

REPORTER. You've come from nowhere, Willy!

WILLY. Please, I —

REPORTER. What was nowhere like?

WILLY. No questions, I —

REPORTER. Tell us about vague obscurity!

WILLY. Let me pass, please, I —

REPORTER. Is it true you're afraid to go out in public?

REPORTER. Is it true you've turned against everyone

who supported you for years?

REPORTERS. *(ad libbing)* Scars! Your scars! We want scars! Show us scars.

REPORTER. Come back!

REPORTER. Is there any sexual significance to that term?

REPORTER. What's your favorite, Willy?

REPORTER. What's your preference, if any?

WILLY. If you'll just —

REPORTER. What do you think of vertical smiles, Willy?

WILLY. Will you please let me through!

REPORTER. Is music a metaphor for life, Willy?

REPORTER. Is life a metaphor for life, Willy?

REPORTER. What is music. Willy?

REPORTER. What is life, Willy?

REPORTER. Are there alternatives?

REPORTER. Are they fun?

REPORTER. What is fun?

REPORTER. We've heard some disturbing rumors, Willy!

WILLY. They're true, Please, I —

REPORTER. One word, Willy. Poignant!

WILLY. Please.

REPORTER. Carry a grudge, Willy?

WILLY. Please!

REPORTER. Are you bitter?

REPORTER. Or don't you care?

WILLY. I've really got to go!

REPORTER. Seen any sights?

WILLY. No.

REPORTER. Heard any sounds?

WILLY. No.

REPORTER. Felt anything worth feeling!?

WILLY. No! No! No! *(sudden silence)*

REPORTERS. We're all just doin' our jobs. Just this one time and we'll be your friends for life. Do you suffer from impotence? Premature ejaculation? Have you slept with a woman of every race. Christ, I bet he has.

ALL THE REPORTERS. Wow! *(They madly write in their notebooks.)*

REPORTER. Fave drugs?

WILLY. I—

REPORTER. *(scribbling)* Willy on drugs! Wow!

REPORTER. Ill feelings?

WILLY. I —

REPORTER. Willy feels bad! Wow!

REPORTER. Regrets?

WILLY. Yeah, but —

REPORTER. Major regrets! Wow!

REPORTER. Sense of loss?

WILLY. I —

REPORTER. Heartbreaking loss! Wow!

REPORTER. Loss of appetite!?

REPORTER. Starving!

ALL THE REPORTERS. Wow!

REPORTERS. *(ad libbing)* Out of my way! Me next! Willy! Willy! Stop pushing! Willy, Willy! Questions! Scars! Scars! Questions! Willy! Willy! Questions! Scars! Willy, Willy! Scars! Questions! *(The REPORTERS are screaming and cursing and grabbing at WILLY. He covers his head and cowers. The REPORTERS surround him like hungry wolves.)*

WILLY. Argghhh! Savages! All a you, savages!

(SOUND! The lead-in to a news program. The reporters step back, growing silent. A MAN steps from the wings. He is in a brightly colored blazer and tie. He holds a mike. He straightens his tie and cues someone that he's ready. The bright LIGHTS of a television camera hit him.)

ANCHORMAN. *(in a huge, orotund voice:)* Hi! Channel Five news and we're here with that man with the bulletproof heart and — I gotta say it — in all modesty, a close personal friend of mine, the incredibly famous Willy Rivers. *(He thrusts his mike at the still cowering WILLY.)* Willy, you are looking some kind of good!

WILLY. I feel good, I feel fast, I feel relaxed.

ANCHORMAN. You heard it, ladies and gentlemen, and you heard it here. How's it feel to be making a comeback, Willy?

WILLY. Like I never left.

ANCHORMAN. That's the hombre we all know and love. Will, you are just looking so good!

WILLY. I feel good. I feel fast. I feel relaxed.

ANCHORMAN. Ladies and gentlemen, this guy is a sweetheart and a real man besides. I wouldn't take you seriously, Will-o, if you weren't. How about a couple for the photographers?

WILLY. Why not?

(FLASHBULBS pop. Cameras click away.)

ANCHORMAN. Is this a classy crew of paparazzi or what?

Wait a sec, lads, wait a sec. Any love interest, Willy? No?
Good. We'll take care of that.

*(He whistles. A breathtaking BLONDE in a tight dress hurries
on.)*

ANCHORMAN. Isn't she lovely? Grab a thigh, dear! *(She
immediately grabs the anchorman's thigh.)* Whoa. No, wrong
thigh, dear.!
REPORTER. Isn't she beautiful? *(She grabs WILLY's
thigh.)*
ANCHORMAN. There we go.
REPORTER. Isn't she sweet?
ANCHORMAN. Little more cleavage, dear, most of these
lads work for family magazines. Great. Love it. When did
you realize it was true love, Will-o? *(The BLONDE puts her
hand on WILLY's crotch.)*
WILLY. Just now.
ANCHORMAN. Is it serious, dear?
BLONDE. *(looking at WILLY's crotch)* It's getting serious
very quickly.
REPORTER. Isn't she delightful?
ANCHORMAN. Kiss her lad! *(But before WILLY can move, a
REPORTER sweeps the blonde into his arms, bends her back and
kisses her passionately.)* Beautiful, we love it, let's go. This is
Channel Five news. Good night.

*(Television LIGHTS dim. Everyone begins Exiting in a
different direction.)*

REPORTER. Page 1! Where's a phone? That's a wrap, I

got what I came for! Let's pack it in, today's news is tomorrow's headlines.

ANCHORMAN. Good luck, Willy. And stay away from people's gunsights, you mad muchacho, you.

BLONDE. *(handing him a slip of paper)* Call me sometime. *(The ANCHORMAN and the BLONDE Exit.)*

WILLY. Savages.

(LIGHT change. The sound of CHEERING, of distant MUSIC. BODYGUARDS enter. They are followed by GOATMAN JANGO. He is a Rastafarian with a huge, long, matted dreadlock. The BODYGUARDS draw their weapons when they see WILLY. WILLY cowers.)

GOATMAN. *(Moves forwards, stands staring, surprised.)* Ah, Jah. Ah, Jah. We need a little sanity, man, am I right?

WILLY. Ladies and gentlemen, the incredibly incredible Goatman Jango...

GOATMAN. Hey! Willy, man, hey, I hear you be havin this comeback.

WILLY. You heard right.

GOATMAN. Hey, man, maybe you some kinda crazy or somethin, right? Shoot me once, shame on you. Shoot me twice, goddam stupid shame on me. Huh?

WILLY. How'd your set go?

GOATMAN. Ah, Jah. We be talkin' whitebread here tonight. I be in dese states united now six months. Lousy, man. Cold. De sun, it be peerin through de haze all de time and it hardly be warmin de blood, man, right? Food be lousy with blandness, de beer be warm and de ganga don't take you no place you ain't been before on a bad day.

WILLY. Good houses?

GOATMAN. Whitebread college kids. On scholarship. Or else sloppy little punks, man, in torn clothes for effect only. I ain't complainin, man. But dis one goddam crazy universe where punk kids can pay thirty dollars to see Goatman or maybe de incredibly famous Willy, and still have the balls to be wearin a torn t-shirt. Right?

WILLY. You know what de hell kinda bloody right.

GOATMAN. De famous Willy. Ah, you be a good soul, Jah. True, true. You play de songs and you take de pay and you never bitch about de breaks. Right?

WILLY. My comeback, man, I'd like you to be there. *(Pause)*

GOATMAN. I be playin, man. *(Pause)*

WILLY. I find myself thinking of a time when the Goatman was in one mean ass white bread joint ... wantin bad to score some rum at the bar. This was in the land of Mississippi, land of pick-up trucks and unbelievers.

GOATMAN. Land where de cowboys wear their hats three sizes too small me think.

WILLY. And who was sittin next to you?

GOATMAN. De beautifully famous Willy. I remember. De cowboy with de neck de color of cherry tomatoes, he be lookin at me, checkin out de locks an de gold an how fine my teeth gleam in de light a de cafe that be dim and seemingly lit by moonlight, man. An he say in this loud voice — I ain't sure I can sit in a joint that serves goddam, crazy looking niggers. I see a course dat he be talkin' about de beautifully famous Goatman, de brainless honky schmuckface.

WILLY. But de Goatman plays smooth and dumb, by Jah!

GOATMAN. Oh, yah! And he smiles so pretty and his teeth gleam like so much shark teeth on sand under Jamaican stars.

WILLY. And Goatman say?

GOATMAN. Sumbitch, pardner, hey! You some kinda crazy fuckin right and if dey serve me any crazy looking niggers I will not eat them!

WILLY. You pissin on me, you smarty pants, dope-wreakin' nigger? *(There is such menace in WILLY's voice that GOATMAN tenses in surprise and then anger.)*

GOATMAN. No, pardner, but maybe I'd like to.

WILLY. *(softly)* That cowboy stood and there was trouble in the air, man.

GOATMAN. Hey, I know. De Goatman smells trouble. Knives, Willy. Guns and razors. Man wantin to see what color de Goatman's blood be. Man, I don't buy it. *(As if by magic, a switchblade appears in GOATMAN's hand.)* De Willy. Oh, de famous, lovely Willy. I see you look up from your tequilla-margarita-old fashioned martini or whatever de hell it is de whitebread drinks, and you say — huh?

WILLY. Sit down, piss ant. Are you so stupid and thick that you don't recognize the incredibly famous Goatman Jango? You touch one strand of his disgustinly matted and putrid hair and they'll be riding your ass out of town on a rail. Right?

GOATMAN. Ha-ha-ha! You know what kind of bloody right! He knew! He knew! Dere was money on the line! Huh?

WILLY. When it comes to the color green, the whole world is bleedin heart liberal.

GOATMAN. Ten minutes later, dat cowboy, he be askin' for the Goatman's autograph.

WILLY. Ten minutes later that cowboy was buying the drinks! *(silence)*

WILLY. I saved your ass. *(silence)*

GOATMAN. An I thanked you for it. I can't be makin your comeback, Willy. *(silence)* My friend, when I hear about you bein' shot to pieces in front of a live audience and cable camers, know what I figure? I figure you came up against one who needed the reknown more then the money. Needed the screams more then the love. I figure it was a cowboy so stupid and thick, he think he be shootin' at something incarnate and real and not something made up by the press releases.

WILLY. You figured right.

GOATMAN. A course. I'm smart. I know dat de world is but a dream, man. Swirlin smoke dat ya take deep and exhale, right?

WILLY. Not right enough.

GOATMAN. No. Oh, so right. *(Takes out his knife. He looks at it a moment. He gives it to WILLY.)* Be kind, man. For your soul's sake. An man ... *(Reaches up and removes his hair. The dreadlocks are a wig and his hair is close cropped beneath it.)* Laugh lots.

(GOATMAN laughs. And WILLY joins in, laughing. But then the laughter seems to stick in his throat. GUITAR riff! LIGHT change. EXPLOSION! A battlefield. The sudden sound of MACHINE GUN FIRE, EXPLOSIONS, the WHISTLE OF MISSLES. A

SOLDIER dressed in bloody combat fatigues and carrying a machine gun comes running on. He "fires", making machine gun sounds the way a child would playing make-believe.)

ACTOR. Rats! Rats! Commie Rats!

(EXPLOSION! He rolls and comes up firing from the hip.)

ACTOR. You killed my brother! You killed my brother! *(He pulls a grenade from his belt and panting with exhaustion, he pulls the pin and throws it.)*
ACTOR. Eat shrapnel, scum!

(EXPLOSION! He leaps for cover and comes up shooting.)
ACTOR. Butchers! Murderers! You're against everything freedom loving men hold true.

(EXPLOSIONS! He rolls and scrambles for cover. SHOOTING. WHISTLING MISSLES. EXPLOSIONS. He pulls out binoculars and peers into the distance.)

ACTOR. Jesus, Mary and Joseph! Wiped out! What is a solitary yankee doodle dandy to do.

(EXPLOSION!)

ACTOR. Assholes! *(He runs for cover and begins returning fire. WILLY has been watching with delighted amusement. He approaches.)*
WILLY. Hey, man.
ACTOR. Hey! The recently internationally-made-famous-

Willy. Que pasa, amigo? *(shouting)* What's up?

WILLY. Not much. Listen, they're planning this big comeback for me and I was hoping you could be there?

ACTOR. A comeback, huh? When's it gonna be?

WILLY. Any moment now.

(EXPLOSION. The ACTOR furiously returns fire.)

ACTOR. You killed my brother! You killed my brother!

WILLY. So what do you think? About my comeback, I mean. I know you're in the middle of this television movie and you're just a little bit busy.

ACTOR. Busy's not the word. *(The ACTOR takes a grenade from his belt and hands it to WILLY.)*

ACTOR. Drop this for me, huh? *(WILLY does.)*

ACTOR. Grenade! Leap on it, Willy, leap on it! *(WILLY does. The ACTOR immediately leaps on top of WILLY.)*

ACTOR. Boom! Willy. Oh God, Willy. You shouldn'ta done it, Willy, sacrificin yer'self for a bunch a ner' do wells like me an the boys. What do I tell your wife, Connie and your snot nosed bambino's Homer and Roscoe? Speak to me, Willy, speak to me.

WILLY. How about my comeback?

ACTOR. Good god, man, there's no time for that now. You seen a tank anywhere, Willy? That's my cue.

WILLY. Gee, I passed a tank back that way.

ACTOR. What? Aw, man. I musta missed it. Where's my bazooka? Aw, man, aw.

WILLY. Tough luck. How are you supposed to wipe out a helpless village without the proper hardware?

ACTOR. Exactly. You don't happen to have a flame thrower on you, do you, man?

WILLY. Hey, I must of left it in my other pants. Can't you use your machine gun?

ACTOR. I guess. God. It's gonna take forever. *(He shoots from the hip.)*

ACTOR. Not bad, huh? Behind the back. Between the legs — you gotta be careful with this one. Eat lead, you god-forsaken religious fanatics!

WILLY. We'll hold onto these oil fields or die trying!

ACTOR. Whoo! Some fun, huh?

WILLY. Yeah.

ACTOR. *(peering through binoculars)* We just knocked out a squadron of Shiite Moslems, opium-crazed and screaming for blood.

WILLY. I want you to come to my comeback cause you're brave, man, I can see how brave you are.

ACTOR. Brave's my middle name, kid. When they need a good man for an impossible mission that no one can return from, I raise my hand.

(An AIR RAID SIREN goes off.)

ACTOR. That's my cue. Excuse me a mo'.

WILLY. Aw, hey, may I?

ACTOR. Shall we shoot them together?

(Together They fire and fire. SHOTS! The ACTOR is hit. WILLY follows suit. They sprawl to the ground. They crawl towards one

another, gasping in pain. WILLY is having to work hard not to giggle.)

ACTOR. I'm hit!

WILLY. I'm hit!

ACTOR. God, I'm hit! Normally this doesn't happen, man. Bad guys are notoriously bad shots. I requested it. I'm an actor, man. Pathos is my bread and butter. I'm shot!

WILLY. Me too.

ACTOR. I'm scared.

WILLY. So scared.

ACTOR. Am I gonna die? I don't wanna die.

WILLY. I don't wanna die. I — *(Freezes. He leaps to his feet, horrified suddenly at what he's doing. The ACTOR clutches at WILLY's ankles.)*

ACTOR. Am I gonna make it, Sarge? Am I gonna make it?

WILLY. Stop it, man.

ACTOR. Medic!

WILLY. Stop it!

ACTOR. My large intestine is wrapped around my ankle like a wreath! I want Mommy! *(He dies. Pause. He sits up.)* God, this fake blood is such a pain the way it gets in your cuticles. So! What'ja think of my death scene? Pretty good?

WILLY. *(softly)* Very realistic.

ACTOR. That's a compliment coming from you, amigo, cause, hey, you've been there.

WILLY. Listen, my comeback, can you make it? Maybe you could come armed.

(There is a DRONING sound. The ACTOR looks skyward.)

ACTOR. Bout time! It's the bombers. I been expecting'm.

WILLY. So listen, can I count on you?

ACTOR. For you, amigo, this busterbrown'll be there. We incredibly famous have got to stick together, am I right?

(EXPLOSION. LIGHT change.)

ACTOR. What the — ? What's that?

WILLY. Looks like a mushroom cloud.

ACTOR. What? Who wrote that into the script? Nobody tells me a damn thing. That must of cost the guys in special effects a bundle. Ah, well, who cares? Time to call it a day.

(A SHOT. The ACTOR falls and is motionless. WILLY forces a laugh.)

WILLY. You guys, you kill me. You're always on. Television movies, man. Jesus. Nobody gets hurt, everybody gets up and goes home. Hey, if this was real, I bet they couldn't get you up off your belly with a backhoe, huh? Hey. My comeback. I can count on you, right? *(and then with realization and growing panic:)* They shot you. They shot him. The star. Somebody shot the star! Somebody is shooting the stars! Somebody is shooting all the stars! Help me! Help me! *(THE ACTOR suddenly springs to his feet, laughing.)*

ACTOR. Fooled ya. Come on, kid. Willy, what's the matter? Come on, dinner's on me.

(He exits, whistling. WILLY stands there looking lost and terrified. LIGHT change. MUSIC. The SOUND OF KEYS turning in a lock. The SOUND OF A DOOR opening and closing. LIGHT as a wall switch is hit. DARLENE gasps and drops her bags of groceries.)

WILLY. Hi, darlin. Didn't mean to startle you. Forget I still have a key? Guess I should have called. Sorry. You look ... so good. Like always. Hey, hey, know something? I'm always thinking I see you at a distance. Uh-huh. Walking a beach. Across a street, waiting for the red. In passing cars. I'll go, like — hey! That's Darlene. Can't be. It is. No. Yes! And I go tearing off in pursuit.

DARLENE. It's not me, is it.

WILLY. It hasn't been yet. And so I make a fool out of myself in front of a strange woman.

DARLENE. I'm sure they don't mind, Willy, when they see it's you.

WILLY. Darlene? You ever think you see me?

DARLENE. No.

WILLY. Would you run for a better look if you did?

DARLENE. *(picking up her bags)* Have you eaten, Willy?

WILLY. Not for days and days.

DARLENE. Are you hungry?

WILLY. There are pangs.

DARLENE. I'll get dinner off the floor and into a pan.

WILLY. Where's the kid?

DARLENE. She has a name.

WILLY. Where's Patty?

DARLENE. At my mother's.

WILLY. Oh. How come?

DARLENE. I'm going away for a week.

WILLY. Oh. Where?

DARLENE. I'm just going away.

WILLY. Oh. Heard I was in town, huh? Where you going?

DARLENE. The Bahamas.

WILLY. Only people I know who go to The Bahamas are dope dealers. You getting into dope?

DARLENE. I've had my share of dopes.

WILLY. Goin' by yourself?

DARLENE. Would you like a beer or a glass of wine?

WILLY. Jesus! Darlene, you still have this bad habit of never lying.

DARLENE. We're not married anymore. I don't have to tell you.

WILLY. If the truth's gonna hurt you either change the subject or you don't say a thing.

DARLENE. I'm not going by myself. (Pause) That shouldn't hurt you.

WILLY. Did I say it did?

DARLENE. You looked like it did.

WILLY. It serious?

DARLENE. Yes.

WILLY. Oh, for chrissake, don't lie but at least learn to fudge a little bit.

DARLENE. You shouldn't care.

WILLY. Did I say I did?

DARLENE. You look like you do.

WILLY. Maybe the kid could stay with me while you're gone.

DARLENE. She has a name.

WILLY. I'm around for awhile.

DARLENE. Willy, she has a name.

WILLY. They have me making this comeback. Too bad you're going to miss it.

DARLENE. She has a name.

WILLY. Patty. O.k.? Patty. Her name is Patty. Can Patty come stay with me while you're off fucking someone in the Bahamas?

DARLENE. No. *(Pause)*

WILLY. Sorry. Sorry, Darlene. I don't know ... everytime I see you, no matter how long it's been, I realize...

DARLENE. What.

WILLY. I realize how much I ... you know...

DARLENE. What.

WILLY. You *know.*

DARLENE. I've never doubted all the time you've loved me, Willy. I've just never been able to handle all the times you haven't. I thought you were dead.

WILLY. Hey.

DARLENE. I was watching the news. They showed the film clip. The women screaming. The men struggling with that guy. You. On your back, your arms and legs at these funny angles and your eyes were open and even on ... even on television I could tell you weren't seeing anything. I was so sure you were dead.

WILLY. What'd you do?

DARLENE. I turned off the set. I took the phone off the hook. I didn't answer the door when people knocked.

WILLY. What'd you do with the — Patty.

DARLENE. I brought her into bed with me that night and I held her.

WILLY. It help?

DARLENE. It helped me.

WILLY. Darlene? You want to see my back?

DARLENE. Is it horrible?

WILLY. No, it's beautiful.

DARLENE. No.

WILLY. Listen, can I ... ? You mind if I sorta ... ? *(He takes her arms and puts them around him. He holds her close. She doesn't resist.)*

WILLY. Squeese a little, will ya? *(With a sigh, She does. They kiss.)*

WILLY. Can we go in the bedroom?

DARLENE. *(a moment)* All right. You can't spend the night.

WILLY. Please?

DARLENE. No.

WILLY. Will you still make me dinner?

DARLENE. Come on.

(She leads him away by the hand. LIGHT change. MUSIC: an acoustic guitar. Shadows up on WILLY. He is sitting, is shirtless. He holds an acoustic guitar. The feeling is that he's sitting by a window looking down into the street. The LIGHTS of passing automobiles play off him. A WOMAN'S VOICE calls out of the dark:)

BLONDE. Willy? Willy?

(BLONDE Enters. She wears a long sheer nightgown.)

BLONDE. Hi. I woke up and you weren't there and then I heard you out here. Watcha doin? Couldn't sleep? Sometimes I, like, can't sleep. It's no fun. You wanna, like try again?

WILLY. I wouldn't be any better than last time.

BLONDE. Oh, it was o.k. It was very good. Really. I mean, I've had worse.

WILLY. I just wasn't in the mood I don't think.

BLONDE. I sometimes am not in the mood. But it doesn't mater if I'm not cause, like, you can't tell and I can just pretend that I am. Oh, but I didn't. Not with you. Oh, no never. You really turn me on and I like you a lot.

WILLY. You hardly know me.

BLONDE. Oh, but I feel like I do. I feel like I've known you forever. I was very excited when you called.

WILLY. I didn't want to be alone. I was with someone and they were leaving town and ... well, I called. I wake you?

BLONDE. I didn't mind. Play me something? *(He shakes his head no.)*

BLONDE. Teach me to play something?

WILLY. Would you like to learn the perfect E chord?

BLONDE. You think I could?

WILLY. It won't be easy.

BLONDE. What do I do? *(He hands her the guitar and forms*

a chord with her left hand.)

WILLY. And your hand goes like this.

BLONDE. Wow. Heavy. I'm getting a cramp.

WILLY. Shake it out, Momma.

BLONDE. You're funny.

WILLY. Strum. *(She does. It sounds horrible.)*

BLONDE. I think I need an amplifier.

WILLY. Press hard. *(She strums.)*

BLONDE. I did it.

WILLY. An E chord.

BLONDE. Wow! Are there any songs in the chord of E?

WILLY. Raise that finger.

BLONDE. *(strumming)* Oh!

WILLY. E minor.

BLONDE. It sounds like ... like...

WILLY. Like a man has lost something and can't find it.

BLONDE. Oh. Well, yeah, I mean, it sorta does ... *(strumming)* No. It sounds like flamingo dancers. It sounds like gypsys. Wow, I'm playing the guitar. I've never been able to play anything before.

WILLY. Sure you have.

BLONDE. No, my boobs have a tendency to get in the way of most normal human activities. You play.

WILLY. I can't. My fingers don't...

BLONDE. Oh. From the ... ? It's a beautiful scar. Does it hurt?

WILLY. There are pangs.

BLONDE. I'm glad it didn't happen to me. I do my best work on my back. You smiled. I saw. Good.

(LIGHTS from a passing car play off them.)

WILLY. You ever wonder who drives cars at night? Maybe nobody. Maybe the cars drive themselves. Maybe they wait till their owners are all in bed and then they go off and meet somewhere and have a big party. Get bombed on high test. Snort motor oil. Caress each other's exhaust pipes. Nine months later the unlucky ones give birth to compacts.

BLONDE. You're not like I thought you'd be.

WILLY. How'd you think I'd be?

BLONDE. Well, adventurous.

WILLY. Like on my albums covers. *(Pause)* Have you ever bought one of my albums?

BLONDE. See, I heard they were making a movie of your life story and all, and I thought you must be sorta adventurous for them to do that. And like, if you have any influence and could set up an audition ... ? Movies are great, you know? Sometimes in movies everybody is sad? Somebody has died or something and everybody is in mourning? Everybody is miserable and they still seem to be having a better time than I ever do. On my best days even. I thought you'd be like that. Having a better time.

WILLY. What do you think now?

BLONDE. I don't know. You're nice but you seem ... sad. *Sad*-sad. Don't be sad. At least you'll always be able to say you were famous for a little while. I'd give anything to be like you. Noticed. Most of us never get noticed for anything. I want more than that. I want ... I want men to threaten to throw themselves off tall buildings if I won't marry them. And when I won't? They do. I'd like to feign humility while all the time accepting important awards. Thank you, everyone, thank you. I'd like to thank ... me. I want ... I want ... I don't know what I want. It all.

WILLY. Look, I'm having this ... you want to come to a ... never mind.

BLONDE. Sometimes people like me but sometimes they seem embarrassed to have me around.

WILLY. No.

BLONDE. It's okay. Thank you for teaching me the perfect E.

WILLY. Keep the guitar. Practice.

BLONDE. .Come to the bedroom. It'll be better this time. I know you now and I won't expect anything. Come on, sweetheart. I'll do it all.

(She kisses him and then exits into the dark. MUSIC. WILLY rises and turns to watch her go. The LIGHTS of a passing car play off him. The scar is like an angry red road down his back. The MUSIC suddenly changes to the guitar riff. LIGHT change. A GIRL enters as if pushed through an open doorway. She is small and pale and her hair is spiked and streaked violet. She wears tattered clothing and leather. She is more frightening than comic, is very attractive in a waif-like sort of way. She stares at WILLY, all challenge, and then, ignoring him, sits on the floor and "watches television." A VOICE sings from off-stage.)

GYPSY. *(off)* It was late last night when the boss came home, askin about his lady.

WILLY and GYPSY. *(WILLY joins in, harmonizing.)* An the only answer he received, is she's gone with Gypsy Davey.

(GYPSY enters. He is a long haired, moustached man in fringed buckskin and cowboy boots and hat.)

GYPSY. Be you the incredibly famous Willy Rivers?

WILLY. I be. An who be you, handsome stranger?

GYPSY. I be the notorious poontanger, Gypsy Davey. Is your dance card filled, you homo?

WILLY. Who leads, ya or me?

GYPSY. *(embracing WILLY)* You, since you're havin a comeback, jack! Whoo-ee, Momma! Tell your daughters to pretend they're wheelbarrows, Willy Rivers gonna drive ... them ... home!

WILLY. How's life, Gypsy?

GYPSY. Sweet potato sweet, boss. You really gonna let'm take a second shot?

WILLY. What am I if I ain't a star?

GYPSY. True enough. What are we without our public? *(He grabs a half full bottle of bourbon from the jacket pocket of the punk.)*

GYPSY. You hear my latest? Jewel encrusted solid plutonium.

WILLY. Any good?

GYPSY. Jesus, faithless women, drunks, pick-ups, shotguns, freight trains and your basic half-wit virgin cousin.

WILLY. An the flipside?

GYPSY. Same thing recorded slower. It be selling, famous Willy, how it sells. Hold it. Wait! Check this out, pardner. Come here, darlin. *(He lifts the punk up off the floor and sets her on her feet.)*

PUNK. How come we don't have this room? I like this

room better than our room.

GYPSY. It's the same room, darlin.

PUNK. The furniture faces in a different direction.

GYPSY. Haw! Ain't she somethin? Don't she make your gonads come to attention? Are we a couple or what? I love her, honest. I can't get enough of her. She's fourteen carrot gold, matie. Watch this. *(Grabbing her roughly)* Ramones darlin. Rock and roll as decadence. Thousand watt Marshall amps in feedback land with the lead guitarist, an acid freak in a mohegan and a tutu, playin a stratocaster with his teeth.

PUNK. Tsk. Take it into traffic.

GYPSY. Haw! Join in, Willy. You and me been there. South a Houston!

WILLY. East a Sheriden Square!

GYPSY. Mud Club!

WILLY. C.B.G.B.'s!

GYPSY. A band named after somebody barfin!

WILLY. Sid Vicious scarfin hisself and his old lady in some fleabag in Chelsea!

GYPSY. Violence!

WILLY. Hate!

GYPSY. Shaved heads!

WILLY. Razorbladed retinas!

GYPSY. Unrest and discontent seethin in the urban cauldron of a youthful wasteland.

WILLY. The bomb!

GYPSY. Boom!

WILLY. Nothing!

GYPSY. Nuclear winter!

WILLY. Radioactive babies!

GYPSY. God is dead!

WILLY. Or wearing headphones and the music's turned to ten! *(They collapse to the floor, exhausted and panting. The GIRL stands there, unmoved.)*

GYPSY. She's gold, Willy, solid gold. She's dyed her bush that color too.

PUNK. Die. Just die.

GYPSY. I ain't complainin, darlin! Took a little gettin used to first time I went carpet munchin but I'm gettin so's I like it.

PUNK. Roll over and die twice.

GYPSY. No. We understand. Don't we, Willy? Way back when he and me joined hands.

WILLY. Grew our hair.

GYPSY. Chanted mantras.

WILLY. Sang protest songs.

WILLY and GYPSY. *(singing)* Kum-bai-ya, my lord, kum-bai-ya.

GYPSY. Passe, darlin.

WILLY. Useless.

GYPSY. Wouldn't make the inside pages a Newsweek let alone the cover.

WILLY. You do what you do.

GYPSY. I hear ya. Couple a years from now though, honey, you're gonna hope that shit washes out. *(Sweeps the punk up and kisses her passionately. He drinks from the bottle of bourbon. Holds the bottle to the girl's lips so She can drink.)* You wanna take this little honey into the bedroom, Willy? She'll give you a ride you won't never forget. *(The PUNK approaches WILLY, sinks to her knees in front of him.)*

WILLY. *(gently)* No.

GYPSY. Here's the key to our room, darlin. Go on back and stick something up your nose.

PUNK. *(to WILLY)* I like this room better. *(She Exits. And now when GYPSY speaks, He speaks in a normal voice with no trace of country accent.)*

GYPSY. Do you think I'm a degenerate?

WILLY. Yes.

GYPSY. Me too. *(GYPSY takes a big belt of booze. He offers the bottle to WILLY who refuses it.)* How are, you, Willy?

WILLY. I'd say terrified sums it up. And yourself, Gene?

GYPSY. *(taking a drink)* Surviving nicely, thanks. Gene. When's the last time anyone called me Gene?

WILLY. When's the last time you spoke like a normal human being?

GYPSY. Long time, Boss.

WILLY. Anybody ever wonder how a boy from Marblehead, Massachusetts picked up a southern accent?

GYPSY. Nope. Neither has anyone asked how a graduate of the Juilliard School of Music seems only able to play three chords.

WILLY. Nobody wonders, nobody cares.

GYPSY. Course not. They just figure the territory comes with the cowboy hat. *(Begins carefully laying out lines of cocaine.)* Chill out, son. It'd be a real mistake to think people take us at anymore than face value When it gets down to basics, celebrity comes in second to the price of milk, bread and ground beef.

WILLY. Why me?

GYPSY. Breakdown in security, I guess. I tell you, there's coming a time when the rich are gonna live in fortresses. Locked doors, armed guards, tanks instead of station wagons. Have versus the have nots, Willy. That's what's coming. You been living in this gilded fishbowl for too long. New York, L.A. T.W.A. It's a jungle out there, son. Most people don't read the newspaper, they *are* the newspaper. You got a guy who works fifty hours a week in a steel mill to feed his kids, he's got no savings, his car is rusting to pieces, his house is falling apart, his son is getting into drugs, his wife is pushing a size eighteen and every time he turns on the tube, he sees people who have what he thinks he oughta have and knows he never will. That can make for some anger, son. That can make for a little despair. That can make you want to shoot somebody. Either that or dance to rock music. *(Takes an enormous snort of cocaine.)*

WILLY. Gypsy? I've been sleeping fourteen hours a day lately. More.

GYPSY. Ah. *(He takes another enormous hit of cocaine.)*

WILLY. It's not the sleep I like. It's the moment before waking. You drift. I could drift forever. *(When GYPSY speaks now, the accent is back full force. It's as if he's shifted from first to fifth gear.)*

GYPSY. I'm givin all this up soon and becomin a surfer I think!! At's a fine obsession, lookin for perfection in a curl a water! *(He takes a belt of bourbon.)*

WILLY. Why'd that guy shoot me, Gene? Why shoot a stranger?

GYPSY. I'm also thinkin strongly on becomin' a marathon runner! I'd look some kinda cute in a pair a sheer nylon shorts and I hear you get high from oxygen deficiency! *(He takes another belt of bourbon.)*

WILLY. Will you stop with that and listen to me!?

GYPSY. Aw, man! Anything you do, if you love it, shit, that's the only reason you need to do it. But ya gotta be careful. People get jealous. You got somethin good, people want to take it.

WILLY. Unless you screw it up yourself.

GYPSY. Hey. Listen, man, listen. *(He sings. The melody is from the aria in "Gianni Schicchi" that the daughter sings to her father. The words are Gypsy's. He's countrified it.)*

OH, MY LOVE, I LOVE YOU
YOU KNOW HOW MUCH I LOVE YOU
YOU KNOW I'LL ALWAYS LOVE YOU
LOVE YOU WITH ALL MY HEART.

(GYPSY stops. Pause. WILLY has turned away in disgust. GYPSY sings again. But this time the melody is pure and clear and the voice is deep and sad and recognizable as a voice once classically trained.)

OH, MY LOVE I NEED YOU
YOU KNOW HOW MUCH I NEED YOU
YOU KNOW I'LL ALWAYS NEED YOU
NEED YOU WITH ALL MY ...

(Pause)

WILLY. Why'd you stop, Gene, that's pretty. You write that?

GYPSY. My next big hit, son. Music by Puccini, lyrics by yours truly, the incredibly notorious Gypsy Davey ... Ah, Christ, fuck me. *(He chugs the bourbon.)*

WILLY. Aw, Gene, look at you, man.

GYPSY. I was gonna be a singer, a real one. I loved to fuckin sing!

WILLY. You don't have to worry about people shootin

at you, you're killing yourself.

GYPSY. Not my fault!

WILLY. It wasn't mine either, man! Oh, man, what I doing here? What am I doing? It's run for the hills time, man! Get out of the line of fire! Get away from the battle zone! Flatuence to flatuence, muck to muck, may we rest in peace. Drink! Nothing means nothing! Stick something up your nose! Nothing adds up to nothing. Take a girl into the bedroom and go for a ride! Sex and death! That's all anyone is concerned with around here! Get fucked and die! Get fucked and die! Just ... aw, man ... you can't help me! No one can! *(Exits, leaving him.)*

GYPSY. Yeah. I don't blame ya. Go. Hide. Till they find you. *(He wets his fingers and wipes up the rest of the cocaine. He licks it off his fingers. Exiting.)* When they do, you gimme a call, son. I'm aroun'. I got lights.

(He hits a switch. LIGHTS to black. The sudden sound of a restless crowd; CHEERS, VOICES, STAMPING FEET. A VOICE speaks out of the black:)

SUIT. Ladies and gentlemen, the incredibly famous Willy Rivers!

(The SCREAMING and APPLAUSE of the crowd is deafening. It's like an arena is being shaken to it's roots by the sound of cheers. LIGHTS crisscross the stage like lazorbeams. MUSIC as WILLY hits the stage.)

WILLY. *(screaming to be heard)* Thank you! Thank you very much!

(The MUSIC changes gears; hard driving, expectant and WILLY reaches for the mike and he sings.)

WILLY.
MAN CAN MAKE THE STAGE DIM.
MAN CAN MAKE THE NOISE STOP.
MAN CAN MAKE A DRUM BEAT.
MAN CAN MAKE A GUITAR WEEP.
MAN CAN MAKE THE ROOM BRIGHT.
MAN CAN MAKE THE DARK LIGHT....
TONIGHT!

GOT ANTICIPATION.
GOT A GOOD CONNECTION.
GONNA MAKE THE JOINT JUMP.
WE GOT A CHAIN REACTION.
GONNA CHANGE THE LANDSCAPE.
GONNA MAKE YOUR HEART BREAK....
TONIGHT!

WE DON'T STOP!
UNTIL WE GENERATE HEAT.
WE DON'T STOP!
COME ON AND CRANK UP THE BEAT.
WE DON'T STOP!
UNTIL YOU'RE DEAD ON YOUR FEET.

MAN CAN MAKE A MELODY.
MAN CAN SET YOUR SOUL FREE.
MAN CAN MAKE YOU LOSE CONTROL.
MAN CAN MAKE YOU ROCK AND ROLL.

MAN CAN MAKE YOU FEEL GREAT.
HOT GIRL ON A BLIND DATE....
TONIGHT!
(repeat chorus)

(Suddenly, from the audience, a MAN runs onto the stage. He dances with the music a moment, his arms about his head in ecstacy. He draws a pistol from under his shirt and He raises it and eE fires. WILLY is hit and HE goes sprawling. The KILLER fires again and WILLY jerks as the bullet hits him in the back. Chaos. MEN run from the wings and drag the gunman away. Feedback. Willy is lying in a pool of blood on stage. SCREAMS. Fade to silence. The LIGHTS on Willy dim to black. The SOUND of an ambulance grows and then fades away. LIGHTS up. WILLY is center, the horror of the memory still with him. SUIT is standing next to him but WILLY is oblivous.)

    SUIT. Willy. Willy, kid. It is time.

(LIGHTS fade to black.)

ACT II

An electric GUITAR screams out of the black, the notes one on top of
another, clear yet unbelievably fast. LIGHTS up on WIL-
LY. He sits, holding the guitar, staring at his hands, unable
to play, the solo now nothing more than a memory. He begins
to awkwardly strum, humming. He talk/sings, struggling
with a melody, with lyrics.

WILLY. There's a boy ... There's a ... boy? There's a ...
Whoo, boy. There's a girl. There's a girl and her hair is
blonde ... brown ... green? And she's dyed her bush that
color, too. Blah. Want to ... what. Take? Shake! No. Eat,
ate? Rotate! Get down, got to town, get a room, get a
wound. Wound.

(Silence. WILLY suddenly bangs, discordant, furious, CHAOTIC
CHORDS on the guitar. SUIT Enters.)

SUIT. Tuning up, are we?

WILLY. *(panting)* Devil with the blue suit on.

SUIT. As of right now, I want you to put all fears
aside.

WILLY. I used to write happy endings, man. Made a
point of it.

SUIT. You do not have to worry about a thing. They are
out there screaming. They are not going to hear a word
you sing or a note you play.

WILLY. I mean, my folks were semi-hip. I got through high school in one piece. I'm not a bad looking guy, I can walk and chew gum at the same time. I always thought people liked me.

SUIT. Like you? They love you. I want you to listen to me. We opened the doors. The crowd stampeded to get in. Teenagers have been trampled. Crushed to death, Willy. It's fantastic. If I'd known it was going to be like this, I'd have contracted some Hell's Angels for security.

WILLY. I guess I always felt an obligation. Hope? Dumb! Bad career move. Critics and academics do not respond to optimism. Light at the end of the tunnel? Lies, man, lies.

SUIT. Are you asking for my opinion? You're finally on the right track. I've heard some of your new stuff. There are the beginnings of a pervasive, black pessimism to it. That and some anarchy. The little necrophiliacs who spend their parents money on records, concerts and bad haircuts, they love anarchy. They love style. Speaking of which, I really would like to get you into some spandex. Skin tight, multihued. Ludicrous. We'll stuff a salami down your leg. The desensitized little mutants eat it up.

WILLY. I can't play anymore, man!

SUIT. And I keep telling you. It doesn't matter. You don't have to. Willy ... this is the first gig! Of the rest of your life!

WILLY. My first gig, man, was in the high school gym. A battle of the bands. Aw, but we were ready. Me and my band even skipped a day of school that week to practice. Mom was going shopping. I kept calling home, waiting for her to leave so we could go over and jam. She'd answer, I'd hang up. Finally she didn't answer. We hit the house, turned the stereo on while we tuned up. Five minutes later cops barged in with drawn guns. Mom had freaked out about the phone calls, decided robbers were casing the joint. Cops had kept an open line on the place, bugged it. We came in and blasted some sergeant into the ozone with Jimi Hendrix, Voodoo Child Slight Return. I got arrested in my own house. Had to do 26 hours of detention. But it was worth it. What dumb kids. We were. Fiddling with our amps that were no bigger than library books. Wa-wa pedal on loan. Four dollar fuzzbox. Feedback mikes. Test! One, two! Wherraughhh! The sound-check was longer than our set. We only knew three songs but depending on the drum solo we could stretch'm anywhere from ten minutes to four hours. Playing. Rock and roll. And all the guys and the girls that we went to school with everyday, the jocks, the cheerleaders, the freaks, the beeries and the druggies, the grease eddies ...everyone listening. Dancing. Bonded together by it. As into digging us as we were into playing for them. Man ... what an innocent time. Playing for friends for free.

Suit. Free? Willy, trust me on this. You'll never play for free again.

Willy. It's gonna cost me, huh?

Suit. You don't understand. You just don't get it, do you? Willy, you are a media myth, shot and almost killed on national television. You don't get much more vital than that. May I tell you something? I wish I had the courage to do it. I bet every nothing, no account, nobody in that audience tonight does too. I want you to get ready now. A river flows through here and it's wild and fast and in places the white water leaps to fifty feet high. And the name of that river is...?

WILLY. Willy.

SUIT. Very good. Let's ease the boredom of paltry, dreay lives, shall we? Willy ... Rock! Lives!

(He Exits. LIGHTS change. The echoing SOUND OF CELL DOORS slamming shut. A MAN skips on like a small, unassuming child. He is followed by a BLACK ORDERLY.)

ORDERLY. Fi' minutes. No mo'. *(The PRISONER approaches Willy. He smiles, shyly.)*

PRISONER. Hi.

WILLY. Thank you for seeing me.

PRISONER. It's a pleasure. I didn't think you'd be able to swing it. You did. I'm glad. Did they frisk him? *(The ORDERLY nods.)*

PRISONER. I wondered. Not that I think you'd try anything. Yes, it's a pleasure and an honor and I've been looking forward to it. *(He holds out his hand for WILLY to shake. A moment. WILLY shakes it.)*

PRISONER. Now we're friends. I have watched you play so many times.

WILLY. You have?

PRISONER. Oh, yes. In my opinion, you're an artist. You always have been. Like me.

WILLY. You?

PRISONER. An artist changes one's preception of reality. I changed yours a lot.

WILLY. You did.

PRISONER. Don't thank me. At the time, changing your perception of reality wasn't my intention.

WILLY. What was your intention?

PRISONER. I was trying to kill you. *(Pause)* However, since death might be considered a drastic change in perception, I guess you could say my intentions have been consistent from the beginning. Artistically speaking.

WILLY. Why?

PRISONER. Why what, Willy? *(He giggles)* That sounds funny. All those W sounds. WhywhatWilly. Why. Because why, that's why.

WILLY. That's not an answer.

PRISONER. I think he's getting violent.

ORDERLY. Don't.

PRISONER. You ever killed anybody?

WILLY. No.

PRISONER. Ever want to? He has. I bet you have. It's great. You're so in control. Of course I'm talking premeditated. You're so ... powerful. You walk down the street and no one knows how powerful you are. You're like God. All you have to do is act and everything changes. You've taken a color out of a painting and substituted one of your own. You've given somebody else's melody different notes. You're a pebble that's been dropped in a pond. Concentric circles get wider and wider. He's getting violent. He's going to hurt me.

ORDERLY. He hasn't twitched.

PRISONER. You watching him?

ORDERLY. *(sighing)* Like a hawk.

PRISONER. When you're capable of killing, you're not afraid of anyone! You laugh inside cause you know that hardly anbody is capable of striking out the way you are. For keeps.

WILLY. But why me?

PRISONER. You look good. People like you. Girls, I bet, like you. I bet they want to fuck you. I bet you have fun. I don't have fun. I never did. Why you? Why not me? Why not me!?

ORDERLY. Cool out.

PRISONER. I was contemplating the President but it didn't look like he'd be passing through town for quite some time. You were elected. *(He giggles.)* I made a pun. I did, I made a pun, huh!?

ORDERLY. I'm e'static.

PRISONER. If you must know, it was nothing personal. When I pulled the trigger I wasn't even thinking of you. No. I was thinking of me. I was thinking of me and what everybody else was gonna be thinking of me.

WILLY. What were they going to think of you?

PRISONER. I dunno but they were gonna and that's something. I'm a pretty far out dude, you know.

WILLY. I'm sure.

PRISONER. Better believe it.

WILLY. I do.

PRISONER. Yup. And so does everybody out there. I have gotten over a hundred death threats! And at least twenty-five proposals of marriage. That's something.

WILLY. It is.

PRISONER. There's a campaign started to free me.

WILLY. I'm sure.

PRISONER. Oh! And I've found Jesus.

WILLY. Where?

PRISONER. Have you always been so cynical?

WILLY. What were you before...?

PRISONER. Before we met? I was a custodial engineer. I worked at a hotel. I picked up after people like you. Televisions thrown from the fourteenth floor in an attempt to hit the swimming pool. Parties. Groupies. I heard of this one girl, she was casting molds of you people? Of your ... things. For posterity's sake? That happen to you? She entice you into a little ... you know ... and then whip out the playdough? Famous people sure do lead the life of Sodom and Gomorrah, huh? Lucky we don't turn to salt. You know, even before I made my initial artistic statement of trying to shoot your lights out, I was interested in the creative process. I mean, right this minute, here and now, are you creating? Is it thunderbolts? Is that how the muse strikes you? I'd really like to know.

WILLY. At this moment, it's like I'm sitting here sifting through garbage and, kerplew, a dove is shitting in my hat.

PRISONER. *(giggling happily)* Kerplew!

WILLY. This nonsense would make a song I say to myself.

PRISONER. Kerplew!

WILLY. Add some violins and some congas and somewhere some drug-adled kid'll dance to it.

PRISONER. Kerplew!

WILLY. Top ten.

PRISONER. Kerplew!

WILLY. Platinum.

PRISONER. Kerplew!

WILLY. Rich as Croesus and for what? It's enough to make you mad. I want to thank you.

PRISONER. Really?

WILLY. Oh, yeah! The things I was concerned with? I wasn't concerned with the things that most people are concerned with. Breakfast, lunch, dinner. No, not me. I was in search of meaningful existence. Thanks to you, now I'm into barely surviving. It makes living risky. It makes it intriguing on a daily basis. Nothing like facing death to make existence meaningful, right? Aw, christ...

PRISONER. Is it time for me to go yet?

WILLY. No! I don't blame you, really, it was my mistake. I spent all my time trying to be famous. I might as well have painted a bullseye on my back. A low profile, that's the ticket. Keep your head down and out of the line of fire. Those who know, those who really control, those who play the pieces, the chessmasters, the suits, they're faceless. They're smart. I wasn't smart at all. My priorities got all screwed up. Creative, special, famous. Dumb! When a person can become famous for something as senseless as pulling a trigger, why try to be famous at all. *(as if accepting an award)* Thank you, yes, thank you, Mom and Dad. It takes a certain sort of imagination to carry off this personal form of creative expression that I am justifiably famous for, don'tcha know. *(He aims his finger at the PRISONER like a gun.)*

WILLY. Kerplew.

PRISONER. *(shooting back)* Kerplew!

WILLY. Yes, it takes a certain sort of non de plume.

PRISONER. Kerplew.

WILLY. A little bit of se le guerre, right?

PRISONER. Kerplew!

WILLY. A little bit of jun o se qua.

PRISONER. Kerplew, kerplew, kerplew!

WILLY. Sheep. All of us. *(The PRISONER bleats — Baaaa-aa! WILLY throws himself at the prisoner and begins strangling him. The PRISONER shrieks like a helpless child. The ORDERLY leaps between them, sturggling to pull WILLY away. He succeeds, throwing WILLY bodily.)*

WILLY. I was a person. I wasn't just a face. I was more than a name.

ORDERLY. Time.

WILLY. No. He doesn't understand what he did.

ORDERLY. Face the fact, Jack. Some people don't.

PRISONER. I gotta go. Listen, I want to mention that I'll be coming up for parole? If you could put in a good word for me, maybe publically forgive me, it'd be a help. Maybe our fan clubs could organize something that would be to our mutual benefit. *(He sticks out his hand. He takes Willy's lifeless hand and outstretched hand. He shakes.)*

PRISONER. Good. We really are freinds. It's been very nice meeting you. Formally, I mean. Don't forget, a word from you would help. *(He skips offstage like a small child.)*

ORDERLY. Looney tunes. This fruitcake costs the state several hun'erd dollars a day. You ax' me, we should dig a ditch, bury fools like him in the dirt up to they necks with only they heads above ground? Then we run over they heads with tractors. Till the ground is as level as a Kansas field. Then we plant wheat. Mental cases like that, it's a sickness, know what I mean? It's catching. Well, off

to the wars. It's all gonna get worse before it gets better.
That's my motto. *(He stops just before he exits. He aims a finger
at WILLY.)*

ORDERLY. Kerplew! *(He exits. Pause)*

WILLY. Only the ball, only the ball, only the ball ...
Friends! I need friends for my comeback! Darlene!?

*(GUITAR riff! LIGHT change. WILLY'S VOICE calling out.
LIGHT to WILLY running on, breathless.)*

WILLY. Darlene? Darlene!?
DARLENE. Willy?
WILLY. Darlene, where are you?
DARLENE. I'm coming!
WILLY. Darlene!

*(A HALL LIGHT is turned on. DARLENE Enters, pulling a
robe on.)*

DARLENE. Willy, what's wrong? Has something happened to — ? *(He grabs her and hugs her desperately.)*

WILLY. Oh, thank christ, I thought you might have
left already.

DARLENE. Willy, tell me what's happened!

WILLY. O.k., listen. You can't go.

DARLENE. What?

WILLY. I want us together again.

DARLENE. What are you talking about?

WILLY. I'm gonna do this one last gig, the very first and
last one and you'll come and you'll be there with me and
then that'll be it. I'll come back here with you and we'll

live here, you, me and Patty —

DARLENE. Is that what this is about?

WILLY. No! We'll go away, the three of us. To the mountains or someplace, way the hell out there where nobody can get us. What.

DARLENE. Have you lost your mind?

WILLY. Yes. No! Everything is fine now. Darlene, I want us together again.

DARLENE. Shall we draw up a contract? One that says when you're finished with me I'm not entitled to your money, your property or your life?

WILLY. No ... hey ... Okay, we'll get married again.

DARLENE. Oh, Willy.

WILLY. Darlene, what are you saying? Are you saying no?

DARLENE. You've got timing, Willy. One thing you have is a sense of timing.

WILLY. Darlene! I need you! *(Again, He grabs her and holds her. Pause)*

DARLENE. Willy ... I remember you saying to me once that if you had to choose between your career and your personal life, you'd want a happy personal life.

WILLY. I said that? Of course I said that.

DARLENE. You never did it. All the choices you made took you away from me.

WILLY. I was making us a living.

DARLENE. I'm not talking about the work.

WILLY. What are you talking about?

DARLENE. Faith. Trust. The lack of it.

WILLY. Darlene ... girls, they just come on to me and ...

DARLENE. I know.

WILLY. You don't. Darlene, I ... I'd get lonely.

DARLENE. I don't think you know what lonely is compared to what I felt.

WILLY. It was always you, is you I —

DARLENE. Love. You never say it. You use it so easily in songs but you never really say it. You're always finding it for the first time or losing it for the last time. You break my heart. It's pretty faces you love.

WILLY. You're pretty.

DARLENE. I'm not bad. But I'll grow old.

WILLY. Gracefully.

DARLENE. Steadily. You'll get bored. You'll want others. You'll get insecure and you'll want to know that others want you. Because of what you are, they will. You'll take them.

WILLY. No.

DARLENE. Yes.

WILLY. Darlene ... believe me when I say I'm through with all that.

DARLENE. I can't. I used to envy you, Willy.

WILLY. Why?

DARLENE. Cause I'm a human being. I'd like people to pay attention and call my name. But I don't envy you anymore. I pity you.

WILLY. Gimme a break.

DARLENE. I do. The attention goads you and pushed you and you're never satisfied with anything you ever achieve. Turn your back on it, Willy, right now. No thinking you're going run away after this stupid comeback is over.

WILLY. Darlene, if you can help me this one time, I can
do it.

DARLENE. See? You want it. You always will. I think you
ought to leave, it's getting late.

WILLY. *(embracing her desperately)* Darlene, after!

DARLENE. Don't.

WILLY. Darlene, marry me!

DARLENE. Willy! You use me. You use how I feel about
you. You care about me but then you leave me and I can't
take it anymore. You feel bad, I know. But then you write
a song about it and you feel better.

WILLY. I never did that to hurt you.

DARLENE. Well, it did.

WILLY. Why can't you ever leave that alone?

DARLENE. You use the people who love you.

WILLY. You were never just something for me to write
songs about, Darlene, and you know it!

DARLENE. I know it? All I know is that when you left
and it just about killed me, you and that friend of yours
turned it into some pop forty hit.

WILLY. You got my royalties! I set it up that way!

DARLENE. I didn't want royalties. I wanted you. Goodbye, Willy. And Willy? I'm changing the lock. *(She
Exits.)*

WILLY. Darlene, I wrote it for you, I wrote it for
you!

(LIGHT change. A VOICE calls out of the dark:)

SUIT. Ladies and gentlemen, the incredibly incredible
Goatman Jango!

(MUSIC! LIGHTS. The sounds of WHISTLES and CHEERS as GOATMAN enters and takes the mike.)

GOATMAN. Hold onto your torn t-shirts, whitebread, cause de Goatman be singin you a song written for him by his friend, close and personal, de incredible Willy. Now de Willy, man, he be havin this comeback and I hope he knows I'd be dere if I could. Dis song is taken from Willy's very own famous life, hey, and his experiences of a famous nature. Right? You know what de hell kinda bloody right! Hit it! *(And He sings.)*
DA DAY WE BROKE APART
MY HEART WENT ICY NUMB
DERE WAS NOT ANY PAIN, NO, NO
JUST A SHOT A NOVACAIN
LIKE DE OCEAN I WAS CALM, BABY
LIKE DE CALM BEFORE A WIND
COULDA BEEN A HURRICANE, OH, YEAH
OR A SHOT OF NOVACAIN
BUT DE DAYLIGHT,SHE QUICKLY RAN
AND DE NIGHTTIME, SHE CLIMBED ON IN
AND I CALLED FOR YOU IN VAIN
AND FOR A SHOT A NOVACAIN
FOR A SHOT OF NOVACAIN
JUST A SHOT OF NOVACAIN
TO EASE DE PAIN
I WILL NEVER HAVE A HOME
AND I'LL ALWAYS BE ALONE.
IT WILL ALWAYS BE DE SAME
JUST A SHOT OF NOVACAIN
YES, A SHOT OF NOVACAIN

A SHOT OF NOVACAIN TO EASE DE PAIN
(He speaks now as the MUSIC plays on.) Willy! I hope you be gettin back together with that pretty wife a yours, man! But if not, just remember! Breakin up, it be tough on de heart but it be easy on de bank account! Right! You know what kinda goddam bloody hell right!

(CHEERS. APPLAUSE.)

GOATMAN. Thank you! Thank you very much!

(LIGHTS fade on Goatman. MUISC fades. WILLY groans.)
WILLY. No more pain.

(The SOUND and flashing LIGHT of an ambulance. LIGHTS to several PEOPLE milling, all of them engaged in hushed conversation. WILLY joins them.)

WILLY. What's going on?
MAN. Friend or relative?
WILLY. What?
MAN. Are you a friend or a relative?
WILLY. A friend. What's going on? Who's hurt?
MAN. We've had a little accident but it's under control.
WILLY. Accident. What do you mean, a little accident?
MAN. Shush. Getting excited isn't going to help anyone.

(MEDICAL AIDS wheel the BLONDE in on a stretcher. She is

unconcious, covered to the neck with a sheet.)

WILLY. Oh, god, no...

MAN. I'm afraid she took one too many sleeping pills.

WILLY. How many too many?

SUIT. About thirty or forty too many.

WILLY. Aw, no ... *(He gently caresses the blonde's hair.)*

WILLY. Hey, come on ... you've got to come to my comeback. Front row center seats.

MAN. She can't hear you.

WILLY. I can see that. Is she going to be all right?

MAN. Yes. We got to her in time.

WILLY. Who found her?

MAN. No one.

WILLY. What?

MAN. She called herself. She had second thoughts. she always does. And she called for help before it was too late and she'd passed out.

WILLY. She's done it before?

MAN. Has a history of it. They've got to get her into the ambulance now.

WILLY. You're going to be o.k.

MAN. She can't hear you.

WILLY. I know she can't hear me!

MAN. Sorry.

WILLY. Why would she do this?

MAN. She left a note. *(He takes a note from his pocket and hands it to WILLY.)*

WILLY. *(reading)* I can no longer bear the disappointment.

MAN. I think that sums it up.

WILLY. She's such a beautiful woman.

MAN. Breathtaking, yes.

WILLY. Other women would kill to be so beautiful.

MAN. I'd imagine so, yes.

WILLY. It makes you feel good just to look at her.

MAN. Obviously she tried to kill herself when no one was.

WILLY. Who the fuck are you?

MAN. I'm her husband.

WILLY. I'm, uh...

MAN. You're Willy Rivers, yes.

WILLY. I'm a...

MAN. A friend of my wife's, yes, I'm sure. It's kind of you to stop by.

WILLY. I wanted to make sure she came to, uh...

MAN. Your comeback, yes, you said. When is it?

WILLY. Any minute.

MAN. I don't think she'll be up to it by then. Well ... I'll tell her you stopped by. It will cheer her up to no end, believe me.

WILLY. Goodbye.

MAN. If you pass any reporters on the way out, be sure they recognize you. My wife would want them to know you're involved.

WILLY. Do you want to come to my comeback?

MAN. You're very kind but there are other things on my mind just now.

(LIGHT change. MUSIC! A CAMERA CREW. WILLY watches the ACTOR, wearing slacks, a sports jacket, a shirt open at the neck

and gold chains around his neck, leaps as if out of an open doorway. He is holding a huge pistol. The CAMERA CREW closes tight as the ACTOR goes into a marksman's stance, aiming out at the audience.)

ACTOR. Aw, right, police, freeze!

(Three deafening SHOTS; the pistol kicks in his hands.)

ACTOR. Three in the ten ring. Who loves ya, baby? *(He suddenly spins, crouches and aims right.)* Grab a piece of the sky, scumbag! The bomb's due to go off in ten minutes. Where's the mayor stashed?

(He fires. He spins, crouches, aims left.)

ACTOR. Twitch and you got a new navel, sweetheart.

(He fires.)

ACTOR. It's not the law I love, it's a simple thing called justice. *(He straightens, puts the pistol in his shoulder holster and salutes the audience with one finger.)*
ACTOR. Aloha.
WILLY. Hey, man, I've been thinking about you a lot.
ACTOR. The incredibly famous Willy Rivers! Que tal, amigo?
WILLY. Listen, my comeback, you're coming, right?
ACTOR. What's this?
WILLY. My comeback. You said you'd be there.

ACTOR. Not me, man.

WILLY. Of course it was you!

ACTOR. Mighta been some hunk who looked like me. A lot of us he men look alike.

WILLY. For christ sake, please, I need some of my friends there.

ACTOR. Friends? We're not friends. We're just sort of famous together.

WILLY. But we've met, we've shaken hands, we've shared talk!

ACTOR. We have? You're right, we have. Hell, by industry standards we are friends. We're dear friends. We're brothers for chrissake! What is it you want, man, name it, I'll do it.

WILLY. Please ... come to my comeback.

ACTOR. Love to, baby. But I'm in the middle of this television pilot. Crime is a nefarious thing, compadre. You have to nip it in the bud. And I do. Thank god that on t.v. it grows fast. Aloha!

(There is the sudden sound of SCREAMING TIRES and then an EXPLOSION from off-stage.)

ACTOR. What the fu—

WILLY. What was that? Oh, my god, that car is on fire!

ACTOR. I don't have my glasses. Is it a Mercedes?

WILLY. No, it's a Cadillac.

ACTOR. Ah, it's just rehearsal then. Probably the culmination of a high speed chase.

(MUSIC that suggests melodrama and on-screen tension.)

WILLY. The driver is burning! He's burning! *(The ACTOR grabs WILLY by the shirt collar and shakes him. The CAMERA CREW closes in.)*

ACTOR. For chrissake, pull yourself together. I know you've seen the underbelly of life but be a man, by Christ, be a man! *(The MUSIC stops. The CAMERA CREW relaxes. The ACTOR claps WILLY on the shoulder.)*

ACTOR. That was beautiful, Willy. You're justifiably famous. You'll get your residual check in the mail. Excuse me while I reload my rod.

WILLY. Was that fun? Did you enjoy it? Do you enjoy this?

ACTOR. You kidding? Something exciting happens every minute. I do more in an hour than most people do in a lifetime.

WILLY. Oh, yeah. All the times you've barely escaped death, I'd think you'd be a traumatized, paranoid psychopath. But are you? No. You're a hell of a guy.

ACTOR. Better believe it. I never go to the bathroom and I have perfect teeth.

WILLY. Are you coming to my comeback or not, you son of a bitch!

ACTOR. Afraid you're on your own, kid. This is reality we're talking about. *(He suddenly spins, crouches and aims.)*

ACTOR. You! Dog breath! What's it gonna be, me or the swat team!? *(He grins and reholsters his gun.)*

WILLY. It's your fault.

ACTOR. Huh?

WILLY. You and this mindless bullshit pretend. You violate violence. You make it this charade that has no meaning or consequence. When a man dies, somewhere people cry for him. *(WILLY suddenly pulls a switchblade and holds it on the ACTOR.)*

ACTOR. Hey, come on, man.

WILLY. When you cut man, he bleeds.

ACTOR. Please, Willy, kid. I'll come to your comeback.

WILLY. Too late. *(He plunges the knife into the ACTOR's stomach. The ACTOR falls to the floor and dies.)*

ACTOR. Why ... why would you want to go and hurt me...

WILLY. Good to see you man.

(He spits on the corpse. There is the sudden sound of another CAR CRASH.)

WILLY. Hey. Look both ways before you cross the freeway. *(WILLY moves away, walking as if in a daze. The ACTOR suddenly giggles and rises. He looks at the audience.)*

ACTOR. What. You thought that was for real? Come on! *(He whistles the theme from The Twilight Zone*. He draws his gun, crouches and aims at the audience.)* That's *Mister* Law Enforcement Officer to you people. Wipe those smiles off your faces. We have ways of making you toe the line, fuck the fifth amendment. *(He fires and fires until the gun is empty.)* I can't say the "f" word on prime time. I gotta remember that. Aloha! *(He Exits. Silence.)*

---

* Cautionary Note: Permission to produce this play does *not* include permission to use this music in production. Producers must procure such rights from the copyright owner of the music.

WILLY. Gypsy ... Gypsy Davey ...

(GUITAR riff! More ferocious than ever. LIGHT change. LIGHTS to the the punk. She sits on the floor, drinking bourbon, the blue LIGHT of the television bathing her.)

WILLY. *(off)* Gypsy? Gypsy, you there?
PUNK. It's open.
WILLY. *(Enters)* Where's Gypsy?
PUNK. Around.
WILLY. Around where.
PUNK. Somewhere around.
WILLY. When's he coming back?
PUNK. Here?
WILLY. Yeah, here.
PUNK. In due time. Wait. *(Pause)*
WILLY. How old are you?
PUNK. Ageless.
WILLY. Why don't you turn up the sound?
PUNK. I like it off.
WILLY. How come you hang around with Gypsy? Why don't you hang around someone your own age?
PUNK. Money.
WILLY. You're into money.
PUNK. Everyone and everything is into money. I'm young but I'm not stupid.
WILLY. There's more to life than money.
PUNK. Hah. You have money, you have it all. If money can't buy it, it's not worth having. Money can't buy you love. Somebody poor made that up. Yes, I'm into money. I'm into people who spend their money. On me.

WILLY. That's all you want, huh?

PUNK. No, that's not all I want. I want to party all day
and rock and roll all night. You'll excuse me, I'm watching television.

WILLY. What are you watching?

PUNK. A silent game show. I love watching what greed
does to people.

WILLY. Where's Gypsy?

PUNK. Around.

WILLY. How'd you meet him?

WILLY. I hung around. I like the music scene; the
booze, the drugs, the hotel suites, the restaurants, the
limos. I like that. The music sucks but I put up with it. It's
amazing how stupid you so-called creative artists really
are. The egos. Unbelievable. How can product have ego?
Does Kellogg's corn flakes have an ego? No. It'll be
around longer too. What you are is making someone
money. That's why they keep you around, kissing your
ass. Money. Art? Art is worth fart. Unless you can sell it.
Then it's a commodity.

WILLY. Where's Gypsy?

PUNK. In the bathroom.

WILLY. Here?

PUNK. He's taking a bath.

WILLY. Gypsy! Yo, Gypsy Davey, it's Willy.

PUNK. *(There is a tremble in her voice.)* He can't hear
you.

WILLY. Why not.

PUNK. He's dead.

WILLY. What?

PUNK. He's dead. He has been for about three hours. He got fucked up, passed out and suffocated on his own vomit. *(WILLY runs off.)* Stupid. He has everything to live for. He was rich.

WILLY. *(off)* Aw, Jesus!

PUNK. Door number three, you fat bitch. Door number three and you're set for life. No. There's nothing but a small bag of dogshit behind door number two. What'd I tell you. Dogshit. Well, don't worry about it. Everybody's laughing at you.

WILLY. *(Entering, phone in hand)* Hello? Yeah, uh ... wait. What room is this?

PUNK. Who knows.

WILLY. What room is this? Well, somebody's dead. In the bathtub. I don't know why.

PUNK. He got sick of it.

WILLY. Hey, shut up!

PUNK. Cool out.

WILLY. Yeah, o.k., send somebody up. I'll wait. *(Silence. He sits. The GIRL moves behind and begins to kiss his neck.)*

WILLY. Don't.

PUNK. You don't like it? *(She continues.)* Look, I need someone. And I'm good. I'll do whatever you want. For whoever you want. But I don't come cheap. What ya say. *(Suddenly she bites hard on his ear. She grabs his hair and pulls his head up and back. WILLY screams.)* What a ya say? Cat got your tongue? O.k., repeat after me. *(singing:)*
I WANT TO PARTY ALL DAY AND ROCK AND ROLL ALL NIGHT! COME ON, SING. *(She pulls his hair hard.)*

WILLY. *(mumbling)* I want to party all day and rock and roll all night.

PUNK. That stinks. Do it again.

WILLY. *(singing)*
I WANT TO PARTY ALL DAY AND ROCK AND ROLL ALL NIGHT!

PUNK. That's good. That's very good. You'll do. *(She sits on WILLY's lap straddling him.)* You're mine now. Mine. *(She kisses him. A moment. And then WILLY kisses her back. His arms go around her and He stands, lifting her. Her legs go around his waist. But suddenly WILLY breaks the kiss and He throws the punk away from him.)*

WILLY. No. Not yet. Not today.

(LIGHT change. GUITAR! CHAOS! LIGHTS to WILLY, frozen, staring into space. SUIT enters.)

SUIT. Would you like to know what your "fans" are doing out there? Half of them are throwing chairs. The other half have lighters in their hands. The impatient little pyromaniacs are going to torch this fucking place in their misbegotten attempts to turn it into chapel services. These people must be the offspring of all the oakies who ever did acid back in the sixties. Damaged goods. You know who pays for damages? I do. *(Pause)* Willy ... please. They're waiting for you. If you only knew the love they're waiting for you with.

WILLY. They want me dead.

SUIT. They want to pay homage.

WILLY. To my memory, not to me.

SUIT. Willy, you are bigger than ever. You are more

famous than ever —

WILLY. Why don't you go out there?

SUIT. Me? They don't want *me*. Nobody has tried to kill *me*. It's you they're screaming for.

WILLY. Jesus, sometimes it's like getting shot to pieces was the best stroke of p.r. anybody could have come up with for me!

SUIT. You do not get press for good deeds. No one buys tickets to see you becuase you're an upstanding member of the community. Survivors grab the spotlight. Hostages. Victims of circumstance.

WILLY. What about my music?

SUIT. May I be honest?

WILLY. I'd prefer not.

SUIT. Tastes and opinions change. In ten years people might think your music — anybody's music — is a bore.

WILLY. Lies! I want lies!

SUIT. In a hundred years they'll think this "music" was never any good to begin with. But you, Willy. You!

WILLY. A stranger tried *to kill* me.

SUIT. It was a stroke of luck. A career-breaker. For christ sake, I — !

(The sound of distant CHANTING. STAMPING FEET. Wil-ly! Wil-ly! SUIT goes into his pocket.)

SUIT. Look, maybe all you need is a little something to give you courage. A little something to ease the stagefright.

WILLY. Like what, a bullet proof vest?

Suit. What is the matter with you? When did you start thinking the worst thing they could throw at you were tomatoes? Willy, it is time. You're going on and you're going to show them miracles. We are going to ascend heights you never imagined. We are going to stand at the top of mountains and look down and the world is going to be at our feet.

Willy. Screaming for me to jump.

Suit. They'll catch you.

Willy. No way. Sacrifice somebody else to'm! Give'm gladiators, man! Give'm two guys in loin clothes going at each other with razor-edged knives! They'll love that! Be sorta like boxing or football but to the death! That'll get'em off the streets and into stadiums where people like you can keep an eye on'm! Talk to the Marines, man! Order up some volunteers! Cause, man, I am not doing it!

Suit. You shit-ass son son of a whore! You are dicking with me! I do not take well to being dicked! I do the dicking here! The only thing more disgusting than some punk who is on the verge of having it all is to hear him cry about it. There will be no refunds tonight. There will be no refunds. You are going on. Oh, yes! You are facing the music. After that, you are on your own. You can sink as deep into oblivion as you want. *(He starts to Exit. He stops and turns.)* Unless, of course, you're good.

Willy. *(Doesn't move. Silence. Soft. Gentle.)* Dad? Dad?

(LIGHT change. An OLD MAN in pajamas, bathrobe, shawl and slippers shuffles on. The OLD MAN clenches a Baseball Digest magazine in his hand. He stares at WILLY, delighted but

uncomprehending.)

WILLY. Hi, Dad, it's me. How you doin, huh? I came
to visit. It's Willy, Dad.

DAD. If ya must know, I root for the Tig's.

WILLY. Huh?

DAD. Detroit. Baseball. You better believe it, Larry!

WILLY. Not Larry, Dad, no. It's me, Willy.

DAD. You gotta love it. You just do.

WILLY. Dad, has the stroke made you senile or are you
just crazy like me?

DAD. I myself could of been a ballplayer.

WILLY. That's news to me.

DAD. It was a matter of balance. There's something
wrong with my inner ear.

WILLY. That's news to me too.

DAD. When I look up, I get dizzy. I fall.

WILLY. No, you don't.

DAD. I do.

WILLY. No.

DAD. I ... I root for the Tig's.

WILLY. Dad? I would have visited sooner but I've been
kind of layed up. Maybe you heard?

DAD. Hold on to your seat and I will tell you of fan
dancing.

WILLY. Aw, Dad...

DAD. There's a group of us, dear friends all. There's
Stink Wilson down toward the Chrysler plant. We call
him Stink because he makes farting noises with his
cupped hands. *(He demonstrates and then giggles happily.)*
There's Funker the Dude and there's Vin Early who owns

the Sunoco station and his retarded brother, Bus, who makes noises that no one can understand and there's Phil and Benny and Dowker. We root for the Tig's! You gotta love it. A gift. You just do.

WILLY. Funny, isn't it? Kids always expect parents to be strong. Parents, good parents, always pretend to be strong. Nothing you don't know, Dad, not a problem you can't solve. When you're a kid you don't appreciate how well grown-ups put on an act. Like they put on a tie. Like they put on a wedding band.

DAD. Once a year we meet. We pile into Benny's Chevy van. We drive and we drink and we're young and we're carefree.

WILLY. You never did that, Dad.

DAD. We drive interstate 80.

WILLY. You were an executive, Dad.

DAD. We're bound for New York City, home of the hated Yankees. We're so young. So carefree.

WILLY. You were a vice-president. You never hung out with guys from the Sunoco station.

DAD. I root for the Tig's!

WILLY. You voted straight Republican your whole life.

DAD. We drive through Queens which is an up and coming ghetto on the outskirts of New York City. We stop at the only White Castle Hamburger stand in the entire metropolitan area. We buy beef cookies! *(He laughs, delighted with himself.)*

WILLY. Whatever you say, Dad.

DAD. I myself have been known to eat 188 of them in one sitting. We order to go.

WILLY. Dad, sometimes you just want someone, someone who cares about you, to tell you what to do.

DAD. We drive to Yankee Stadium. We're young. We buy right field general admission tickets. Carefree! We sit there, alone in a sea of pin stripe tattoos and crazed Long Island accents. We wear our Tiger colors with pride!

WILLY. They want me to make this appearance, Dad. I don't know if I can.

DAD. Hold onto your seats and I will tell you of fan dancing!

WILLY. Yeah. O.k., tell me.

DAD. High, high in the stands we sit. We drink Yankee Budweiser but we scream for Stroh's. Benny chews tobacco and Phil eats peanuts, the shell and all. Funker the Dude plucks his fake pewter flask from the inside pocket of his imitation mohair blazer and we drink gulps of Fleischman's. So young! Stink Wilson is farting trumpet loud and Dowker starts throwing beef cookies at the right fielder. Carefree! Vin Early is doing an a capella version of "Take Me Out to the Ballgame" and his retarded brother, Bus, starts bawling along, starts bawling something totally unintelligible and incredibly loud and contagiously retarded, starts moaning and gurgling as if in tongues, and suddenly he leaps to his feet and wails like a wolf calling to the moon, urging on, urging on and we join in, all of us. We do it cause we love it, ya got to, ya just do! And then ... and then ... *(The OLD MAN suddenly seems confused.)*

WILLY. Dad, what then?

DAD. I ... I ... I root for the ... *(The OLD MAN'S mouth works soundlessly. He stares at WILLY in anguish.)*

WILLY. What?

DAD. I'm lost. I'm lost. I'm so alone. I'm afraid. *(The OLD MAN weeps.)*

WILLY. It's time, Dad. Dad? It's your turn.

DAD. But what do I do? I don't know what it is I do.

WILLY. You ... Dad, you ... you climb to the top of general admission. Yeah. Higher and higher to where the air is thin and clear.

DAD. I can't.

WILLY. You can. We'll do it together. You know what we do? We grab hold and we pull ourselves up and over the top to the stadium's edge.

DAD. And then?

WILLY. And then we stand. *(The OLD MAN slowly stands.)*

WILLY. So proud.

DAD. So tall. We look down.

WILLY. The cars and buses are like children's toys.

DAD. We look back. *(awed)* Oh.

WILLY. The stadium lights surround us like small suns.

DAD. Thin it is, our path, like the crease on a mountain top. But we're young. We're young. I dance. *(The OLD MAN begins to shuffle to some silent, inner music. He looks expectantly to WILLY who stands quietly. A moment.)*

WILLY. Yeah, Dad. I dance too.

DAD. Fan dancers.

WILLY. I dance for the fans. For the fans do I dance.

DAD. How glorious a gift.

WILLY. Security is screaming and police are charging. There are sirens and screams and bright edged beams cut the night sky.

DAD. I am the focus. I am the fulcrum.

WILLY. I am the fan dancer.

DAD. The game has stopped. The world has stopped. All eyes are on me. And for a brief precious moment, I make the fans forget.

WILLY. I dance.

DAD. *(thrilled)* Oh!

WILLY. For the fans do I dance.

DAD. And the fans cheer me. They cheer hard and long and loud and true. They cheer as if cheering for themselves for once. Don't look down, they cry! Don't look down, they call! Don't look down or back or behind or you will fall! *(The OLD MAN spreads his arms as if in ecstacy.)* I will not look down, say I! I will not look down, I call! I will look nowhere but up ... at the madly swirling stars...

WILLY. Tonight.

DAD. Tonight.

(The OLD MAN throws a triumphant fist in the air and He rears back and He looks straight up. There is the echo of a crowd CHEERING and LIGHTS seem to dance off him and stars seem to come out overhead, surrounding him like a halo. He grows dizzy. He sways. He staggers and falls. WILLY catches him.)

WILLY. Dad!

(The LIGHTS return to normal. Silence. WILLY and the OLD MAN seem equally confused.)

DAD. I root for ... I root for ... *(He caresses WILLY's face tenderly.)* I root for the fans.

WILLY. I do too, Dad.

DAD. I root for ordinary people.

WILLY. I do too, Dad. I do too.

(WILLY helps the old man to his feet. They hug. DAD walks slowly off into the dark. LIGHTS change.)

WILLY. Hold on to your seats and I will tell you of fan dancing. The moment before you grab the light is an age long. Your heart is engine loud in your ears and your gut is like a log jam. You can aim your thoughts anywhere. You can take your eyes and toss them out into the night and they turn and look down on you. You seem to hear a voice pleading. I can't, I can't, I can't. You can and you will, a voice answers. Forgotten, a voice cries, not this time. Can't, can't, crazy, crazy, run, run, run now, hide, yes, no, yes. Go. And suddenly your feet are moving and the light breaks over you and you're aware of a presence. Watching. Waiting. There to be transported with you. You gotta love it. A gift. You just do. And so ... you dance. *(Pause. And then, softly:)* Don't shoot me. Oh, dear god, please don't let them shoot me.

(LIGHTS to black. The sound of CHEERING. Out of the darkness, a voice:)

SUIT. Ladies and gentlemen, it is our very great pleasure to introduce to you ... please, let's all let him know how glad we are to have him back ... a real welcome

for ... Ladies and gentlemen, the incredible ... Willy
Rivers!

*(MUSIC! LIGHTS up on WILLY, his back to the audience. HE
turns, mike in his hand, and he sings.)*

WILLY.
THERE'S A GIRL AND HER HAIR'S PAINTED PUR-
    PLE AND GREEN
THERE'S A MAN IN A CHAIR WITH AN OLD
    MAGAZINE
THERE'S A GUY IN A TUB AND HIS BLOOD'S
    TURNING COLD
THERE'S A WOMAN ON A STRETCHER WHO'S
    AFRAID OF GROWING OLD
THERE'S A BOY IN THE BIG HOUSE AND
HE THINKS HIS LIFE'S JUST FINE
AIN'T AFRAID A GOD ALL MIGHTY, AIN'T AFRAID
    A DOIN TIME
PUT A WEAPON IN HIS HAND AND HE'S A MAN
    AMONG MEN
HE'LL TAKE YOU THROUGH THE VALLEY
AND HE'LL WALK YOU BACK AGAIN.

YEAH, THEY ALL WANT TO TAKE YOU
THEY WANT TO GRAB YOU BY THE HEART
THEY WANT TO WRING YOU OUT DRY
THEY WANT TO NEVER LET GO
TILL YOUR CHEERS AND YOUR TEARS AND YOUR
    HANDS
TEAR THIS PLACE APART

TILL YOUR CHEERS AND YOUR TEARS AND YOUR
   HANDS
TEAR THIS PLACE APART

THERE'S A BOY WITH A GUITAR
AND HIS HEAD IS FILLED WITH DREAMS
HE DOESN'T NEED A SPOTLIGHT
HE'S GOT A PAIR OF OLD BLUEJEANS
SOME SAY THE BOY IS GIFTED
SOME SAY THAT HE'S DERANGED
THE KID PAYS NO ATTENTION
ALL THAT MATTERS IS THE STAGE

WHERE HE CAN TAKE YOU
HE WANTS TO GRAB YOU BY THE HEART
HE WANTS TO SWING YOU UP HIGH
HE WANTS TO NEVER LET GO
TILL YOUR CHEERS AND YOUR TEARS AND YOUR
   HANDS
TEAR THIS PLACE APART
TILL YOUR CHEERS AND YOUR TEARS AND YOUR
   HANDS
TEAR THIS PLACE APART

THIS BOY WAILS...
THIS BOYS FLAILS...
THIS BOY SINGS...
WE'RE GONNA ... GENERATE HEAT ...
(speaking) Thank you very much.

(LIGHTS to black)
END OF PLAY